— IN THE —
RESTAURANT

— IN THE —

RESTAURANT

SOCIETY IN FOUR COURSES

CHRISTOPH RIBBAT

Translated by
Jamie Searle Romanelli

PUSHKIN PRESS

Pushkin Press
71–75 Shelton Street
London, WC2H 9JQ

In the Restaurant was first published as *Im Restaurant* in Germany, 2016
First published by Pushkin Press in 2017

The translation of this work was supported by a grant from the Goethe-Institut

10 9 8 7 6 5 4 3 2

ISBN 978 1 78227 308 0

Text designed and typeset by Tetragon, London
Printed and bound in the United States

www.pushkinpress.com

CONTENTS

I

Opening Times

F rances hurries through the crowds of Chicago. She is looking for a job as a waitress. The trams screech in her ears, a policeman's whistle shrills, the 'L' train thunders. She is thirty-seven, a teacher by training. She started off in a village school with just one classroom, near St Clair in Michigan, right out by the Canadian border. She has lived in the suburbs of Detroit, in the suburbs of Chicago, and then in Great Falls, Montana. That was when she married William and stopped teaching. Then the economy in Great Falls collapsed. They moved back to Chicago. And William became incurably ill. In her threadbare black dress, Frances battles her way through the crowd of people in dark, narrow Van Buren Street. She has seen a job posting in the *Chicago Daily News*. Now she stands in front of the restaurant. She looks in through the window at the bright, decked tables, at ladies and gentlemen eating at leisure, white-aproned girls holding plates in their hands. Frances hesitates. Should she go in or not? Her heart is beating so fast, she writes later, that she almost can't breathe. But she enters eventually, and asks the man behind the cigar counter whether they need a wait-ress. Yes, he says. They did. But they hired one just yesterday. I see, says Frances. She flees back on to the street, back into the hubbub of the year 1917.[1]

*

The Chinese capital is famous for its restaurants. Fish and seafood are excellent here, as are beef, poultry and noodles. The choices are many and varied, because the restaurants aren't just catering to long-established residents, but also to the refugees who now call this their home. Their traditions and dietary restrictions – for example those of Muslim residents – enrich the diversity of the local cuisine. The sweet soy soup at the market comes highly recommended. Also worthy of mention are Mother Song's fish soup and rice served with mutton, while in front of the Longevity and Compassion Palace, meat cooked in ashes is on offer. The boiled pork at Wei-the-Big-Knife at the Cat Bridge is outstanding, and the honey fritters from Zhou Number Five by the five-span pavilion are absolutely exquisite. This is all according to a gourmet. In the year 1275 he writes about the impressive gastronomic scene in Hangzhou, the capital during the Song dynasty.[2]

*

The history of the European restaurant begins with the fact that people aren't hungry. Or at least, they act as though they aren't. In Paris in 1760, with all its malnourished inhabitants, it wouldn't be in keeping with the zeitgeist for the elite to stuff themselves to bursting point in some tavern or inn. Anyone with any sense of decorum has a delicate constitution. Unable to stomach much, they barely eat a thing, but still take their time about it. The upper-class clientele are enticed by the restaurant, this luxuriously furnished new style of inn. Large mirrors in which to admire oneself and others hang on the walls. The 'restorative' bouillons which lend the new restaurants their name, derived from the Latin *restaurans*, steam from decorative porcelain bowls. Made from poultry, game or beef stock, these brews are said to replenish the strength of those who are too sensitive for other forms of nourishment.

It is not the bouillons which make the restaurant successful, however, but rather its focus on individuals and their desires. Customers here don't have to sit at a long, shared tavern table with all sorts of strangers. They get a table all to themselves. They can decide the hour at which they wish to be served. They make their choices from a menu.[3] After the revolution, representatives of the National Assembly come to Paris from the provinces, and go out to eat together in restaurants. The Parisians emulate them. Before long, establishments begin to open which are also, fashionably, called restaurants, but more reasonably priced and less plush than the prototypes. In the revolutionary era, the guild system begins to ease its grip. Gastronomes now have more freedom to satisfy their customers' varied desires. And from the very beginning, service is of great importance for the restaurant's success. Enlightenment philosopher Diderot, for one, after dining out in 1767, praises the bouillon, the iced water and the beautiful *restauratrice*.[4]

*

Out in Van Buren Street, in front of the restaurant with the bright tables and smart waitresses, Frances, rejected would-be waitress, briefly feels relieved. But then she has to make her way onwards, to the next establishment that has placed an ad in the *Daily News*. She is just one of countless women in Chicago who are competing for jobs. She has often thought about these crowds of women, crashing into the heart of the city from the outskirts each morning like a tidal wave. Many are young, some already middle-aged, making themselves look younger with make-up and overly short skirts, while others are simply old, not even attempting to feign youth. An army of women: secretaries, hairdressers, textile workers, daughters of farmers and daughters of factory workers. They are cheap labour, because they are women and because they have no experience when it comes to life and work in the big city. The most visible female workers serve behind the expansive windows of the restaurants – of which Chicago now has over a thousand.[5] And Frances wants to be one of them.

So she moves on. In the next restaurant, a woman is standing behind the cigar counter. She sends Frances on to a young man, who, in turn, refers her to a gentleman in the backroom, the manager, who is sorting aprons and jackets. She asks him whether he needs another waitress. He asks her whether she has worked as a waitress before. She lies and says yes. He asks her whether she is quick on her feet. She asks him whether it looks like she's not. And then another young man leads her down a narrow staircase into a damp, foul-smelling cellar. Here, ten young women are getting changed, putting on lipstick, sweeping rouge across their cheeks, powdering their noses, tossing make-up brushes back and forth and cursing with a crudity that Frances has never heard before in her life. No one pays any attention to her at first, but eventually one of the quieter girls helps her get into her uniform. Frances is now a waitress. A waitress with a secret.

*

On the surface, the early Parisian restaurant resembles the cafés in which bourgeois public life develops. People come together in the cafés. They debate. They argue. Everything is very different from church or the royal court, different from the elite salons, the academies or scholarly societies. Anyone who can pay for his drinks and his food gets in. Anyone can join in the conversation. Newspapers are scattered around, supplying opinions. No authority intervenes, ends disputes or keeps order. If an argument arises, then eventually – or at least so one would imagine – common sense prevails, and the argument reaches a conclusion.[6]

But the restaurant is different. You don't go there to debate with others, nor to read the newspaper. You go to unwind or to put your sensibility on show. Once seated at the table, you make a choice that has little bearing on the broader political situation: between poultry, game or beef bouillon. The blend of public and private life sought here leans more towards the private. The Parisian café offers large rooms in which you can see everything and everyone. The restaurant, on the other hand, has niches and alcoves for customers to retreat into – groups and couples alike. There are *cabinets particuliers* – special rooms in which one can conduct private conversations or meet for assignations ranging from the romantic to the erotic.[7] This is not the place for intense public discourse. And it's important to note: men and women appear together here.[8] A very unusual occurrence – at least for the non-French around 1800, who speak of it with wide-eyed amazement.[9]

*

This is what Frances Donovan isn't telling her colleagues: she wants to become a waitress for research purposes, not because she needs the money. With William being terminally ill, it has become clear to her that she will have to make her way through life alone in future. So she has decided to get another degree. She is studying English at the University of Chicago – with a minor in sociology.

The Chicago School of Sociology is becoming world-renowned. In these early days, Frances is a part of it.[10] The professors challenge their students to use the entire city as a laboratory. They urge them to investigate all facets of urban life: from migration to family life to youth crime.[11] To focus on how newcomers to Chicago are either fitting into the city or foundering in it. Methodical reflections are of little importance to the Chicago sociologists of this time. They seek to break free of the ceremonial character of academia. Their goal is to experience, observe and record, in the moment.[12]

Frances Donovan is so impressed by these concepts that she herself becomes a sociologist. A freelance one, so to speak. Without any contract, position or research funds, she sets out. And in the wilds of the new Chicago, there is no figure more interesting to her than that of the waitress. In 1917, Frances becomes one of them. One year later, in 1918, William will die of his incurable illness. And two years later still, in 1920, a Boston press will publish *The Woman Who Waits*. It is the first academic study of the modern waitress, written by Frances Donovan.

*

Before long, Parisian restaurants of the late eighteenth century are filled with the scent of more than just bouillon. There's chicken and macaroni, compotes and crèmes, eggs and confitures.[13] The Véry brothers' establishments specialize in oysters. Café Hardy makes a name for itself with grilled meats. The Trois Frères Provençaux serve southern French cuisine, cooking with olive oil instead of cream, bringing the bouillabaisse to Paris. By the early nineteenth century, this new type of eating house has firmly established itself, in Paris – and only in Paris.[14]

The era of the restaurant critic is dawning. Alexandre Balthazar Laurent Grimod de La Reynière publishes the *Almanac of the Gourmand*, releasing new volumes regularly throughout the first decade of the nineteenth century. Grimod is tremendously successful. Writers have turned their attention to food before, of course. But it is new for the emphasis to be exclusively on the culinary and on a world peopled only by consumers and chefs.

Grimod invents the gourmand. This new cultural figure wanders the streets of Paris, gazing at the sweets in window displays, pursuing the scent of roasted meat. He recommends little red-breasted robins as a delicacy. He compares the *pâtissier* Rouget to the playwright Racine. He praises Theurlot's butter and the macaroni at Corazza and at Magasin d'Italie. A typical Parisian, he claims that although the best meat may come from the Poitou or Auvergne regions, it only really takes on flavour after it has been delivered to the capital. No topic is too trivial for him. His almanac even addresses how best to sweep away crumbs from the table. He visits and evaluates restaurants, and claims to be able to ruin the reputation of an establishment with a single sentence. Grimod also develops a new type of customer for the post-bouillon restaurant. The gourmand is no longer too sensitive or fragile: as delicate as his palate may be, this customer is healthy and strong.[15]

Writers such as Grimod, Carême and Brillat-Savarin transform the physical act of food consumption into an aesthetic and intellectual practice.[16] Their readers are curious to discover an increasing variety of pleasures. And so two aspects of nineteenth-century society cross-fertilize one another: gastronomy and the expanding world of Parisian journalism. French cuisine only becomes French cuisine because so many people are talking about it.[17]

But great as the curiosity of these dedicated restaurant visitors may be, the kitchen remains closed to them. Only waitresses and waiters cross back and forth between the consumption and preparation areas. For everyone else, the glittering sphere of culinary refinement remains clearly divided from the steamy production space. This is what the success of the restaurant rests upon. It creates illusions. The Véry brothers, for example, famed for their oysters, call their inn Chez Véry, to make you feel you're in their home. But that is most definitely not the case.

Not all customers are able to cope with this. In a restaurant called Véfour, in 1839, former infantry officer Alphonse Robert hurls a wine bottle against a mirror when the waiter refuses to put it on a tab. It is a very expensive and highly symbolic scene, and one which leads to a sensational trial. By throwing the bottle, the officer destroys the illusion of elegance and ease constructed at Véfour. But then again, the fact that the waiter brings the bill at the end of the meal destroys the fantasy too.[18]

*

Frances Donovan wears a uniform now. She belongs. A colleague shows her how things are done. Five barstools at a counter right at the front: this is her area. She has the lunchtime shift, from half past eleven to half past two. First, the customer is given a glass of water, cutlery, a napkin. Then he orders. Once he receives his order, a card is punched. If he orders more, the card is punched again. The first customer has already arrived. He wants ham on rye and coffee. She spots the coffee. But where can she get the rye bread and the ham? Frances whispers her question to a colleague in a white jacket. Back there, he says, you have to call it out. He calls it out for her. The sandwich appears. Now everything is clear to her. She calls for sandwiches. She knows where the coffee is, where the milk is, doughnuts, cake. Then someone wants the roast beef special. It's not where the ham on rye is. In the Foundry, says another waiter. Where's the Foundry? At the back. She hurries off. The Foundry is full of sweating cooks, and in front of it waitresses are shouting orders. The roast beef special comes with mashed potato and a little mound of spaghetti, and the fat, cross-eyed cook slices the roast beef and tells her she should take thirty cents for it. Back to the table. Someone wants hot milk toast. Frances yells out 'hot milk toast' into the Foundry, but hot milk toast, says the fat cook, isn't from the Foundry, but the Laundry. Not back here, up the front. She hurries to the front. Frances yells 'hot milk toast' into the Laundry. Correct. And so it goes on, from the Laundry to the table, from the table to the Foundry and back, napkins, cutlery, glass of water, coffee, and in the midst of it all a customer with a red neck tie stares at her lustily and wants to talk. She doesn't want to talk, most definitely not. Her colleagues help her. They advise her to keep leftover scraps of bread and butter for herself, to take a dirty glass when she can't find a clean one, and not to let herself be caught doing it.

The second day comes and goes. The third comes. Before their shift, in the changing room, the waitresses share stories about men. One girl pulls up her skirts and shows the others her white silk stockings and yellow silk suspender belt, stolen from her landlady, who she claims will never find out. Then comes the hectic lunchtime shift. Men come, men go; most of them want meat, coffee and cake. Sometimes there will be a handsome and better-dressed one ordering a cream roll or a chocolate éclair. The revolving door never stands still, the customers push their way in and back out again, the waitresses serve, clear, run to the Laundry, to the Foundry, fetching napkins, a glass of water, cutlery, again and again. The manager

17

whips a cloth after them, driving them on, the waitresses cry out 'Coming through!' to carve their way through the crowded space – until, on the fourth day, a gentleman appears at Frances' counter and orders bread, butter, peach slices and black coffee. Frances serves him. The manager shouts out that she should bring the gentleman some cream for his coffee. Frances says that the gentleman doesn't want any cream, the manager says that she should bring the gentleman some cream regardless, she says again that the gentleman doesn't want any cream, then the gentleman himself says to the manager that he doesn't want any cream. The gentleman eats and disappears. The manager says to Frances that she shouldn't contradict him. Frances contradicts him again. And the manager fires her. He tells her to give him her apron, right away. She takes it off and presses it into his hand. Then she goes down into the cellar and gets changed.

Her colleagues rally round her. They tell her that she'll find another job without any trouble. They stroke her arm and compliment her on her beautiful waist, saying that they noticed her beautiful waist every day, and her brown eyes too, so pretty – and Frances is almost moved to tears.[19]

*

In the early 1850s, a man named Spencer runs a restaurant on the Mississippi. The eating house is located on a boat, moored alongside Cairo, in the state of Illinois, right where the Ohio and the Mississippi flow together. Here is the border between the South and the North, between the slave states and freedom. Another decade will pass before this world is changed by the Civil War.

Spencer is a free black American. Not a slave. A businessman. And an excellent cook. A contemporary observer explains his talent as 'one of the instincts of his race'. He calls Spencer's establishment a 'restaurat', which could either be a typographical error or a sign that, in the year 1854, Cairo, Illinois, is a very long way indeed from Paris.

For travellers on the Mississippi, the main transport route through this part of the United States, Spencer's restaurant boat is an insiders' tip. White gastronomes in the area are less enthused. To them, Spencer is unwelcome competition. They plot against him and drag him into a lawsuit. He is ordered to appear before the Justice of the Peace. And he does, bringing with him a cask of explosives and a pistol. He makes it clear that he will fire the weapon into the cask if things don't go his way. Afraid of a suicide attack, the Justice of the Peace lets him go. But the white people of Cairo gather on the riverbank in front of Spencer's boat, wanting to destroy his restaurant and drive him away.

Spencer draws his weapon and fires. He shoots eleven people, killing three. The crowd fight their way on to the boat, set it on fire, cut it loose. As it floats away downstream, Spencer appears on the roof, holding in his hand a part of the stove, the heart of his establishment. He has tied the metal part to a rope and slung the other end round his neck. He screams out his contempt to the people on the riverbank. Then he jumps into the water, and the section of oven pulls him down into the depths.[20]

*

The name of a restaurant in itself tells a story. One of the first eating places in Paris is called Le Grande Taverne de Londres, in an attempt to capitalize on late eighteenth-century French Anglophilia.[21] Meanwhile, the first dining establishments in Sydney are called Trois Frères Provençaux and Café Restaurant de Paris, transporting the customers, at least for the duration of their meal, to the gourmet metropolis on the other side of the globe.[22]

The name is not the only textual component involved; the menu is also of key importance. Late nineteenth-century gastronome Julius Behlendorff clearly sets out how it should be handled. He recommends keeping the menus on tables at all times, and declares it to be 'highly inappropriate' for a waiter to pull one out of his pocket. Behlendorff also advises an ambiguous equilibrium whereby the menu should 'not be too extensive, but neither too short'. His advice to heed the close connection between text and reality, however, is unequivocal. It makes a 'bad impression' if the menu is not 'clean and new every day', and would lead any customer to presume 'that the dishes, too, are from previous days'.[23]

The written word also ventures beyond the restaurant itself. In Delmonico's, the most prestigious establishment in New York, head chefs become prominent authors. In 1890, Swiss-born chef Alessandro Filippini publishes a compendium of his recipes with the pedagogical subtitle *How to Buy Food, How to Cook it, and How to Serve it*.[24] His colleague, Frenchman Charles Ranhofer, goes on to surpass him; in 1894, he releases a monumental cookbook entitled *The Epicurean*. It is so detailed that, according to his unimpressed successor Leopold Rimmer, it reveals 'all the secrets' of Delmonico's kitchen.[25]

In the homeland of the restaurant, the tyre company Michelin publishes its gastronomic guide for the first time in 1900. At this point, they haven't yet started handing out stars. One has to actually read an entry before making culinary decisions. Literary figures, too, discover the Parisian gastronomy scene as a setting.[26] Émile Zola's novel *The Belly of Paris*, published in 1873, becomes essential reading for gourmets, portraying the market halls as the fragrant heart of the city.

Now, around the turn of the century, novels and plays are set in dining establishments, and travel articles depict the dishes, the decoration, the spectacle. Only the very select few can afford to dine in sophisticated restaurants, but they are, according to Rebecca Spang, 'in the view and in the imagination of all'.[27]

*

Frances Donovan doesn't give up. She looks for her next job, going from restaurant to restaurant, collecting rejections. Finally, she finds another position. On the second day, she takes the wrong door into the kitchen and collides with another waitress. A tray crashes to the floor and she is fired. And so the search begins again. Her next job is in the spectacular Café of Reflections, where there are mirrors everywhere – on the ceiling, on the walls, on the columns in the middle of the room. The tables are made of glass, the chairs are white, the lights dazzling. Frances spills soup on to one of the customer's hats. After five days, she is given her notice.

Over a period of nine months, Frances Donovan will work in fifteen different establishments. She gets fired again and again. Sometimes for answering back, sometimes, as she herself admits, because she simply isn't a very good waitress.[28] And so she gets to know all the different types of restaurant in Chicago. There's the *hash house*, open night and day, where men can quickly fill their bellies. There's the *tea room*, clean, attractive, with salads and sandwiches on offer, for ladies and a higher class of business people. Restaurants of the finer variety are called 'cafés' in Chicago. Donovan, however, considers these differences to be irrelevant. When it comes down to it, she states, no customer, not even the most upper-class one, has the faintest idea who is preparing the food. She declares that cooks are 'the lowest type of men' to be found in the big city, considering them to be the 'scum'.[29] And she also claims that, while the kitchen of the chic Hayden Square Tea Room may seem very sanitary at first glance, at night it is frequented by rats, some of which are the size of small cats. They wander across dirty plates; rat mothers with their children, on the hunt for delicacies.[30]

*

Cold cuts and bread, and beer in a pewter tankard to wash it down: that's what's on the menu if you go out to eat in late nineteenth-century London. It's the kind of thing you would order in the *chop house*, an old British institution. Or you might hurry out during your lunch break to get a sandwich and a glass of milk. Around 1900, however, these customs are pushed out by a new kind of dining space, now imported from Paris. The steadily increasing number of tourists, the office and shop workers, the theatre folk and their audiences: they want more than cold cuts. The restaurant is more distinguished than the traditional inns. Or more exotic. Or both.

This makes things both interesting and complicated. The new London restaurants are run by the French, by Italians, by the Swiss. Many of the waiters are Italian, Polish or German. The menus in the more lavish establishments are, of course, written in French. So it's not uncommon for a foreign waiter to get muddled up between French, English, his own native language and the complex culinary specialities on offer. This obstructs the dining experience for British customers. To make matters worse, some Londoners suspect the Italian food they're getting is not as good as, and above all much more expensive than what Italian diners are being served. And to top it all off, English waiters are fleeing in the face of foreign competition. Many of them head for New York.

Nonetheless, the cosmopolitan restaurant grows in popularity. The capital of the Empire profits from the colonies; in an increasing number of establishments, the food being cooked is Indian. The South Asian chefs exude competence at the stove and onlookers take note of this, impressed. Around the turn of the twentieth century, an Indian restaurant begins to offer a delivery service – a very modern concept – to all households that can be reached on the Underground. The manufacturer of Nizam Madras Curry Powder has at its disposal a chef who offers on-site classes in Indian cooking to any 'hotel, club or restaurant'. Even an Italian restaurant begins to offer veal cutlet in curry sauce (a critic praises its 'distinctive excellence'). In London, one can now consume Chinese and Malaysian dishes, Greek pastries and Nigerian soup. As the new century begins, the erstwhile capital of cold cuts experiences globalization both on the plate and in the belly.[31]

*

At this time, gourmets find high-end cuisine in the restaurants of large palace hotels.[32] Twice daily, hundreds of guests are catered to there: with luxurious dishes from the French tradition. In 1889, the Savoy opens in London, in 1895 the Palace Hotel in St Moritz, in 1897 the Vier Jahreszeiten in Hamburg. This is where the European and American super-rich come together to feast and be seen. And the upper echelons always eat the same thing, regardless of whether they're in London or St Moritz. Caviar and lobster are ever present. Intense sauces slosh across the plates. Distinguished head waiters flambé crêpes Suzette. Blue flames flicker, smoke rises heavy with the scent of liqueur. According to the wife of the hotelier César Ritz, this evokes 'a feeling of proper respect' in the guests.[33]

The badly paid cooks in these palaces remain invisible and are shown no respect at all. They work fourteen, fifteen, sixteen hours a day. Most of them die before reaching forty, due to the excess of physical stress their bodies are subjected to. They toil in windowless, barely ventilated kitchens. Chefs have more vocational illnesses than miners. They suffer from a chronic lack of oxygen, tuberculosis, varicose veins and – ironically – malnourishment.[34]

This is the world Georges Auguste Escoffier comes from, and now he sets to work reforming it: in the restaurant dining rooms as well as the kitchens. His *Guide Culinaire* of 1903[35] declares that food must look like food again.[36] In this era of ornamentation, his belief that everything on the plate should be edible is novel. And yet Escoffier is no culinary revolutionary. He is simply unable to turn his back on the heavy sauces. But he allows himself to become increasingly inspired by simple French country cuisine. The composition of the dishes must be comprehensible, the customer must be able to recognize the ingredients. Escoffier invents a multitude of new, creatively named dishes. He develops the dessert Peach Melba and dedicates it to the actress Nelly Melba. The 'consommé Zola', made with white truffles, he baptizes in honour of the great novelist. The 'suprême de Volaille Jeanette', a cold chicken-based delicacy, he names after a ship which sank during a polar expedition. He bemoans the fact that there is no copyright protection for new culinary developments.[37]

First and foremost, however, Escoffier is a theorist of the division of labour. In his kitchen, there are precise responsibilities: the *rôtisseur*, the *saucier*, the *pâtissier*, the *gardemanger*, the *entremetier*. Previously, it took one single cook a quarter of an hour to produce 'Oeufs Meyerbeer'. In the Escoffier kitchen it takes just a few minutes for the *entremetier* to prepare the eggs, the *rôtisseur* the sliced lamb kidneys and the *saucier* the truffle sauce.[38] The newly organized kitchen is cleaner, better ventilated, brighter and safer for the men who work in it. Above all, that work is quicker and more efficient.

Escoffier gets right to the heart of why this is so important. The restaurant clientele of the early twentieth century no longer have time at their disposal. The restaurant owner cannot count upon a 'feeling of proper respect' towards his establishment. His waiters can flambé to their hearts' content, but the attention span required for long mealtimes and elaborate dishes is no longer a given. Modern diners, says Escoffier, only have 'eyes for one another', not for the plates.[39] Once again, the point has been reached where the majority of restaurant-goers have barely any interest in the food.

*

Frances Donovan may speak about rats and dirt and reputed human 'scum' in the kitchens. But in truth all she cares about are the waitresses: the girls from the changing room, the warm-hearted warriors with their crude manners and stolen undergarments. She tells of young women who take off their wedding rings in order to get more tips. She knows that the slowest servers can be found in the department-store cafeterias and the prettiest in the so-called cafés. This is also where the wages are highest; the waitresses wear the latest fashions, silk stockings, the finest pink undergarments.[40]

Frances is fond of her colleagues, apart from those who steal her pencil or her tips. And yet she sees things through the eyes of an academic. Or rather, through the eyes of the woman she happens to be: a fair bit older than the average waitress, educated, from the upper-middle classes, a woman who feels superior to the waitresses. She considers herself to be more virtuous. The restaurant girls, she criticizes, read almost nothing but the murder cases in the daily paper. She calls her colleagues 'ignorant' and 'coarse'. She observes that they are actually ashamed of their work, that they would like to come across as sophisticated, but that their bad English always gives them away. 'There's nothing very complex about the waitress,' she concludes in the closing pages of her study. 'Her behaviour can be reduced down to the two fundamental appetites of food hunger and sex hunger.'[41]

In the changing rooms, she takes a close look at her colleagues' bodies. She gazes upon bared chests, fresh skin, and wonders how many of these sexually-so-active young women suffer from syphilis. She quotes statistics from the year 1915, in which the waitresses of Chicago led by a large margin the ranking of professions with the highest incidence of sexually transmitted diseases.[42]

After nine months in diverse restaurants, however, Frances Donovan is no longer able to hide her amazement. 'She is often unwashed', she writes of the typical waitress, 'and her teeth are unfilled, but she knows life and she is not afraid of life, to her it is big, dramatic, brutal but vivid, full of colour.'[43] To her, the waitress is a free spirit.[44] She goes out into the world and fights her way through it: Donovan respects this. The waitress is completely different from the kind of woman who 'comes running with a smile to greet the husband when he rings the bell' in the evening. And so she praises the 'striking personalities in this vulgar Bohemian group', and sees the waitress as part of a feminist movement demanding freedom for all women.[45]

*

Guido Ara from Cologne, Germany, wants to help waiters. Whether in restaurants, cafés or hotels, they need to be able to speak foreign languages. Tourism is taking off and international business contacts are increasing. But waiters don't have time to attend language courses. German waiters may be able to get by in English, concedes Ara, but not other world languages. And so he promises the readers of his books that 'with a little effort', they will be able to pick up the Italian and French they need in just eight days.

Ara's method is simple and accessible. It covers not only the written language, but pronunciation too. 'Zheu voo a-por-tay leh kart deh van too-de-sweet', the waiter can promise the customer after reading Ara's book. He can comment on the services he offers: 'Vo-a-sea vo-tra shap-po'. And he can also announce the recommended dishes: perhaps the 'pee-yeah de-voh sos rem-o-lad', perhaps 'ern bif-stek o pom-sso-tay' or 'ern kart de dan rot-y a-vek marm-e-lad de pom'? When Italian guests come in, he can also offer specialities such 'do-eh sal-seetchy kon krow-ty' and understand when they query the accuracy of the bill – 'Cam-a-yer-ee chay un air-ror-ay nel con-to.' The French sound different: 'Gar-son,' they say, 'ill-ya une er-ror don leh noot.' A German waiter who can respond to that is the 'modern waiter' to whom the author introduces himself: Guido Ara, gastronomy and language expert, five years before the start of the First World War.[46]

*

He would let himself be killed in this restaurant. He would allow himself to be massacred 'without any resistance whatsoever', because he feels a unique 'sense of joy' here. He becomes a completely different person, totally carefree. In these rooms, he lives entirely in the present, is 'no longer [his] grandmother's grandson', as he puts it, but the 'brother of the waiter' who serves him and his companion. He is in a state of ecstasy. Granted, the beer he drinks here plays a part in it too, along with the champagne and the port, but so does the orchestra with its march music, waltzes, opera melodies and music-hall chansons, and the beautiful Princess of Luxembourg, who greets him and utters a few melodious words in his direction, and the tall and spindly head waiter who reminds him of a macaw at the zoo, and the 'sporty gait' of the other waiters, who, despite their haste, manage to deliver the chocolate soufflés safely to the tables and present the lamb chops and steamed potatoes to the customers in exactly the same arrangement in which they left the kitchen.

This is what impresses him most: how the seemingly hectic chaos reveals itself, upon closer inspection, to be a world of order and harmony. To him, the tables full of customers seem like planets, and the waiters around the tables like satellites, bringing wine, hors d'oeuvres, glasses. The serving staff hurry around and cross each other's paths without pause, and he sees the 'regularity of these dizzying yet structured rotations' in the intoxicating system of the restaurant.

He actually feels 'sorry' for the 'other customers', he says. They only think about the person they happen to be eating with, or about how high the bill will be or the fact that they will be coming again the next day. They don't see the tables as planets and the waiters as satellites. Their imagination does not stretch to the kind of thinking with which one can transform the everyday world. But he, the narrator of Marcel Proust's *In Search of Lost Time*, does possess this strength of imagination – and he feels it with particular intensity when he dines with his companion Saint-Loup at the restaurant Rivebelle.[47]

*

What counts as a restaurant in the first decades of the twentieth century? The elitist, aristocratic establishments soon move aside, and the middle classes begin to take over. In Berlin, Aschinger's Bierquellen are multiplying: dozens of fast-food restaurants distributed across the entire city. They offer beer sausages and potato salad. Fresh rolls are complimentary. The company's central base produces the dishes on an industrial level: 2 million pairs of beer sausages in the year 1904 alone. The Aschingers invent a device which can cook 942 eggs simultaneously. The spice mortar has an electric mechanism. Colour enhancers like 'spinach green', 'sauce brown' and 'crab red' lend a hand with the visuals. But this mass production and culinary uniformity doesn't necessarily guarantee automated behaviour from the clientele: in 1907, the writer Robert Walser observes that even in the standing-only Aschinger fast-food places, people seem to 'let time drift away' in a 'downright facetious' manner. He smears brown mustard across his sandwich, drinks a Helles beer, then another, and concludes: 'We're all human, after all.'[48]

In New York, where the restaurant was a bastion of all things French and aristocratic, haute cuisine becomes just one option amongst many. In 1918, an expert counts fifty different types of establishments in which New Yorkers can fill their bellies.[49] These include the automat, a German invention.[50] As early as the 1870s, a new, cost-efficient delicacy emerges in America: it is not as tough as some steaks and consists of meat which has been shredded then put back together again. Its name, initially at least, is Steak Hamburg.[51]

Before this, everything was straightforward. The best food was to be found in luxury hotels. Now, in the early twentieth century, the situation has become confusing. There are restaurants everywhere. As to how good they are, there's no way of knowing. Written accounts become even more important than before. You read up and inform yourself first, then go out. Marcel Rouff and Maurice-Edmond Sailland travel all across France in their quest to produce the twenty-eight-volume culinary guide *La France Gastronomique*. The success of their work can be attributed to the country's automobilization. And they also collaborate with the SNCF, the French railway company. Sailland, known by the pseudonym 'Curnonsky', speaks of the 'holy alliance of tourism and gastronomy'. He creates an index of categories for the establishments he reviews. They range from the 'high-end' via the 'bourgeois' to the 'regional', right down to the 'country kitchen'. It is from this index that the Michelin star system is developed.[52]

Supposedly sophisticated onlookers don't think much of these gastronomic guides. In 1921, one Charles J. Rosebault laments that true gourmets have become a 'lost tribe'. In the *New York Times* he remarks on the presence of 'barbarians' in restaurants. He even encounters people who want 'jazz with dinners'. And he claims that culinary masterpieces are disappearing: down 'indifferent gullets'.[53]

*

The Woman Who Waits is published in 1920. By now, Frances Donovan is making a living as a teacher again. Her position in academia is located somewhere between marginality and invisibility. But she does collaborate with sociologists at the University of Chicago. There's Harvey Zorbaugh, for instance, who is working on his book *The Gold Coast and the Slum*. Zorbaugh, who is to become an influential sociologist, refers to her as a friend and colleague who generously shared the results of her research with him. The academic journal *The Survey* publishes a review of *The Woman Who Waits*, criticizing

Donovan for paying too much attention to the waitresses' sex lives. The sociologist Paul Cressey, however, makes use of Donovan's observations about the sexual strategies employed by waitresses in the workplace. He is researching the taxi-dance halls of Chicago, where women rent their bodies to men for ten cents a dance. These practices are not too far removed from waitressing as Donovan depicts it.

There isn't much more evidence of Donovan's academic reputation.[54] The University of Chicago's sociology programme aims for more pronounced professionalization. There's increasingly less contact between the recognized members of the department and those who don't officially belong. In addition, the male sociologists are pushing their female colleagues out of the programme. They are shunted off into a special department for social services, and subsequently referred to as 'social workers'. From 1920 on, only men are sociologists, and these men are engaged with the sociological study of women. That's how things have been arranged.[55]

Frances Donovan, woman and sociologist, doesn't give up. She gets to work on her next book. Now she researches the 'saleslady', again without any research funds. In the school summer holidays she leaves Chicago, heads to New York, and works in department stores there: Macy's, Bloomingdale's. She conducts her research for two summers, then writes her book. In 1928, it is published by the University of Chicago Press, and receives positive reviews, including one in the *New York Times*.

And it seems as if Frances receives a further accolade. Robert E. Park, the great pioneer of urban sociology, has agreed to write the introduction for her book on the saleslady. Wonderful news – except that, in his contribution, Park somehow manages to dismiss her work rather than praise it. On two occasions he asserts that Donovan's study is not a 'systematic treatise'. He evaluates the book as having 'more the character of a personal narrative', as 'impressionist and descriptive'. Park cites with respect his male colleague W. I. Thomas and the latter's works on the 'adventurous character of women'. But of the adventure-hungry sociologist Donovan, he says: 'Although she may succeed in capturing "intimate insights" she is not particularly interested in the "sociology of contemporary life".'[56]

Once again, Frances Donovan refuses to be knocked down by the slight. She simply writes another book. After studying waitresses and saleswomen, she now moves on to teachers. This, her third monograph, will be published in 1938.[57]

*

Joseph Roth hears tins clattering and water dripping. He walks into a long, narrow, steam-filled room, furnished with wooden tables and illuminated by 'deathly-tired light bulbs' which look like 'stars that are about to die out'. The journalist is visiting the First Viennese Soup and Tea Establishment. He writes about this soup kitchen in the newspaper *Der Neue Tag*. He approaches the poor people dining here with a strange, almost schizophrenic gaze.

First and foremost, he sees ugliness. Heads rest upon 'collarless, bare, emaciated necks', he writes, as if 'impaled there haphazardly'. He marvels at 'grisly and transparent-looking' ear lobes and conjectures that perhaps the poor 'always have such thin ear lobes'. Their noses 'are plump like shapeless lumps of plasticine' which 'no-one has made any effort' with. He looks into eyes that protrude as though 'on stalks' and into eyes that are deeply embedded 'as though ashamed to be on public view'. He notices large, square chins on the men and crooked, slanting ones on the women. Their fingers seem 'gnarly and gout-ridden' and remind him of 'woodland roots'. When he observes them all together, gathered round the tables eating, he registers 'dull, fly-like human lumps'.[58]

Joseph Roth, born and raised in Galicia, has recently immigrated to Vienna. In the early 1920s, he is just starting out as a journalist, but he establishes himself quickly. He composes over a hundred newspaper articles in the space of a year.[59] Although he may conduct his research in a soup kitchen, he does the actual writing in other establishments: primarily in Café Rebhuhn, a coffee house in Vienna's Goldschmiedgasse. In the evenings, he retreats to Café Central or Café Herrenhof. According to his biographer, this is where he becomes 'a serious drinker'. But while he may write in an intoxicated state,[60] his aims as an author are not excessive. Roth declares that he is not interested in the 'monumentality of the whole'. Instead, he wants to give an account of contemporary life by looking at the very smallest of details.[61]

Roth may or may not have been under the influence when he describes the sober carefulness of how they eat in the First Viennese Soup and Tea Institution. He observes how one eater sets down the soup bowl 'carefully, carefully' so that 'not a single drop jumps into the air'. Roth concentrates on how he takes from his bag a spoon 'freckled with rust', how he uses it to eat the vegetables and the soup – only to end up drinking out of the bowl after all. 'The spoon', Joseph Roth theorizes here, is 'just a suffix from the culture of poverty.'[62]

*

In 1922, Edward Hopper paints *New York Restaurant*. An elegant couple are depicted sitting at a table by the window. She is seen from behind, he from the front. The image of this narrow room, filled with people, tables and decorative plants, is dominated by the rear view of a waitress. She is bending over to pick up a tray, her behind decorated with an absurdly large white apron sash. When commenting on this picture, the first restaurant scene of his career, the artist says that he wanted to capture the 'crowded glamour' of a New York restaurant during lunch service. But he hopes that 'ideas less easy to define' also became part of his picture.[63]

Automat is the name given by Hopper to another of his paintings, created in 1927. A woman in a red dress, green coat and yellow hat sits alone at a round table, staring into her coffee cup. The self-service restaurant is bright and bare, decorated only with a bowl of fruit: wax fruits, it seems.[64] Two years later comes *Chop Suey*, depicting two women at a table in a Chinese restaurant. They are attractive, but puppet-like.[65] In 1930, *Tables for Ladies* follows. Here, too, the image Hopper creates seems frozen. There is no hustle and bustle or interaction to breathe life into the scene. In 1942, he produces *Nighthawks*; it shows a simple café, with an employee, two men, and a woman at the bar. Sixteen years later he comes back to the theme again, painting *Sunlight in a Cafeteria*, with a woman and a man at different tables. In this, Edward Hopper's last restaurant painting, only the light and architecture are important. The life in the café is secondary: 'crowded glamour' is no longer in evidence.

Almost always, food and drink are absent; both in the earlier, more lively pictures, as well as the later, more static ones. Hopper's restaurant-goers sit in front of empty bowls, empty glasses, empty plates. The basket of fruit in *Automat* is only decorative. In *Tables for Ladies*, items of food can be seen, but far away from the customers depicted. In *New York Restaurant*, a man is moving his hand. Perhaps he is about to pick something up, or eat something concealed from view by his companion's back. But it's more likely that he's placing

coins on the table, tip money for the waitress with the monumental apron.

Hopper barely differentiates between leisure time and work
in his paintings, depicting offices and restaurants in a similarly
bleak and austere way.[66] The artist's admirers may believe him
to be a realist, but what they get, according to critic Walter
Wells, is just a reduced version of reality. It functions like a
distant memory. The consistently empty plates and bowls,
too, suggest that sensual fulfilment always lies in the past or
the future, but never the present.[67]

*

Eric Blair has moved to Paris to become a writer. He is living
in Rue du Pot de Fer, close to Rue Mouffetard. Each day, he
passes by the cafés and restaurants of the Latin Quarter. On
one occasion, he thinks he sees James Joyce sitting in Les Deux
Magots. In his first Parisian year, 1928, Blair writes a novel.
It is rejected by publishers and he destroys the manuscript.
Eric Blair is part of a mass migration to Paris. The franc is
weak, the city is cheap. Artists, writers and dilettantes are all
flocking to live in the intellectual capital of Europe. Americans
fleeing prohibition head there en masse. They search out the
establishments they have read about in travel guides and in
Ernest Hemingway's novels.[68] In some quarters of the city Eric
encounters more so-called artists than normal working people.
There are 30,000 painters in Paris, he says, and he believes most
of them to be 'con artists'. He himself becomes seriously ill,
recovers, writes some short stories, sends them to a publisher.
The latter declares that they contain too much sex. After that,
the contact fizzles out and along with it Blair's literary career.

Eric needs money. And he wants to stay in Paris. So he
becomes a kitchen hand, in the restaurant of the luxurious

Hotel Lotti near Rue de Rivoli. Three days in, he is almost fired for having a moustache. In Parisian gastronomy, only the chefs have moustaches. The waiters don't, and this subsequently means that *plongeurs*, the kitchen hands at the very bottom of the hierarchy, aren't allowed moustaches either, for this would make them superior to the waiters. The chefs, in turn, have moustaches in order to demonstrate their superiority over the waiters. Eric Blair sees no logic in this. But he shaves and keeps his job as a *plongeur*.[69]

*

In a hotel kitchen in early 1929, Joseph Roth encounters a chef who impresses him. He paints a vivid picture of him, describing the 'brownish red of his cheeks, the metallic shimmering black of his thick bushy brows and the golden brown of his small and alert eyes'. He sketches his 'red lips', 'red, bloodshot ear', 'soft, broad chin', 'wide nostrils', and his 'placid and amicable' belly, inside which Roth suspects exists a 'second, special heart'.[70] Roth is visiting a kitchen made of Dutch tile, glass and metal, which he describes as 'the engine room of a modern ghost ship'. He is here conducting research for a series of articles on the modern nomadic existence, entitled *Hotel World*, for the *Frankfurter Zeitung*. Even more than the restaurant, the hotel is a temporary home. Roth does not romanticize this world. He emphasizes the artificiality that defines all hotels. On several occasions he underlines the fact that the hotels he visits belong to incorporated companies and that the creation of the illusion of 'home' is part of a commercial venture.[71]

Roth is less critical when he catches sight of the chef in the kitchen. He sees him as a figure of 'calm, ease and magnificent indifference'. This chef, according to Roth, is 'as hard-working as a Czech, as thorough as a German, as imaginative as a Slovakian and sharp as a Jew'. If one of his young assistant cooks brings him a dish to sample, he casts 'one of his swift, golden glances' at it and tastes it with the 'valuable tip of his tongue'. After the chef himself has eaten, 'very tiny portions, which lay on the plate like gemstones', he drinks a glass of cognac and then stands up, 'light and free', as if he had sat down that morning by the edge of a forest and is now walking cheerfully towards the rising sun. In his white uniform, the chef seems to Roth like 'a figure from the dreams of [his] childhood'. He embodies 'ceremonial, joyful, substantial, tangible optimism'.[72]

*

One can set one's watch by the cook's meltdowns. She has her first at around eleven in the morning, while preparing the lunch dishes. Then she collapses again at around six in the evening. Then again at around nine. She sits down on the waste bin and weeps. She bemoans her fate, saying that she doesn't deserve all this, especially not after having studied music in Vienna. Afterwards, she drinks a beer and calms down again. She is Eric Blair's colleague in the newly opened Auberge de Jehan Cottin.

The year is 1929. To its guests, the Auberge probably seems very charming. The restaurant is designed in a Norman style. Country-style pottery is placed around the room. Artificial logs adorn the walls. Back in the kitchen, there is a centimetre-thick layer of trampled food remains on the floor: potato peelings, bones, fish tails. A shack in the courtyard serves as a larder, to which cats and rats have free access. There is no hot running water in the kitchen. Plates are washed with cold water and scraps of newspapers. The drain blocks up once an hour.

Eric Blair, the sickly young writer from England, has switched from Hotel Lotti to the Auberge. Here, too, he finds himself on the lowest rung of the power ladder. He works from seven in the morning until midnight. He de-scales herrings, cleans pots, washes plates, dices vegetables, runs errands, sets mousetraps. His work is accompanied by never-ending insults from the cook. And Eric gives as good as he gets. 'Fetch me down that pot, you idiot!' – 'Get it yourself, you old whore.' That's a typical exchange. In the narrow kitchen, the cook's broad hips bump into him whenever she moves. She is endlessly reminding him that her aunt is a Russian duchess.

He is absolutely sure that this restaurant must be the worst, filthiest establishment in the world. But his colleagues tell him that it's even worse elsewhere. He soon learns the ropes. Why wash the dishes when you can just wipe them on your trousers? Out front, in the dining room, no one knows what's going on in the back. The waiter tells him about his predilection for wringing out a dirty tea towel over a bowl of soup before he serves it to the customer. That's his way of exacting revenge on the bourgeoisie. Eric finds out why the Auberge is doing well (which, in other words, means it is frequented by actual French people and not exclusively by tourists): the owners bought sharp knives. That's the secret. If the customers' places are set with sharp knives, any restaurant can become a success.[73]

Eric Blair's gastronomic experiences are good in one respect, at least: they flow into the first book for which he manages to find a publisher. It comes out in 1933. For his pseudonym, he decides on George as the first name, because his father has a habit of calling vague acquaintances George. The inspiration for his surname he finds in English geography: in a village near Cambridge and a river that flows through Suffolk.[74]

*

These children come in, time and time again, and they always buy half a dozen hamburgers at once. They look affluent, different from the usual clientele. Usually, only regular working-class people buy his burgers. Walt Anderson, owner of four fast-food stands, observes them and starts to wonder. So, one day, he follows one of these well-dressed little customers round the next street corner. And he sees a big limousine. The mother inside it, like many other supposedly posh people of Wichita, Kansas, is too embarrassed to be seen buying hamburgers. So she sends her offspring.[75]

The restaurant-chain concept is well known in the United States by this point. Anderson runs a very small chain. But for serial gastronomy to catch on in a big way, there's still one thing missing: a dish which everyone can agree upon. For a long time, American eating habits have been defined by ethnic identity. Only now, between 1920 and 1930, in a modernized, mobile, mass-media society, do these differences begin to dissolve. The United States turns into a homogeneous consumer nation. And the hamburger plays a pivotal role in this process, standardized and mass-produced by the company White Castle: America's first fast-food chain, originating from Walt Anderson's four burger stands in Wichita.

The company erases the hamburger's image as an embarrassing, potentially germ-infested food of the lower classes. It expands, naming itself the 'White Castle System of Eating Houses'. Each restaurant looks the same: a white, quasi-medieval pseudo-castle. 'The era of dirty, greasy hamburgers is over,' announces one of the managers. 'A new system has come into being: the White Castle system.'[76]

In individualistic America, the company's philosophy has surprisingly collectivist traits. White Castle's promotional material reminds the customer that he is 'one of many thousand'. Each and every guest sits on the same kind of stool and at the same kind of counter as everybody else. His coffee is prepared according to a predefined, consistent formula, just as it is for everybody else. The hamburger is cooked at exactly the same temperature for all customers alike. White Castle's aim is not to make the gastronomic experience more egalitarian, more democratic, but rather to emphasize again and again the cleanliness and safety of suspect minced beef.[77] To make this even clearer, America's first big fast-food chain pays a medical student to live on nothing but water and White Castle hamburgers. The experiment lasts thirteen weeks. He eats between twenty and twenty-four burgers a day. And according to management, the student remains 'in good health'.[78]

*

Two other American students, Mary Frances and Al Fischer, arrive in Dijon in 1929. They have just got married in the United States. Al plans to study literature in the French city, and Mary Frances wants to study art. They have brought piles of books with them. Still in the honeymoon period and intoxicated by each other, they want to celebrate their three-week wedding anniversary with their first French meal. They just need to find a restaurant, a good one. Their landlady gives them a small note. They are to give it to Monsieur Racouchot, in Aux Trois Faisans at Place d'Armes. They set off on their way. All they find is a drab little café. They hand over the note. The waiter laughs and leads them into a courtyard, through a door, up a dark staircase, past toilet doors and noisy kitchen rooms and an office, to a small square dining room.

There are no more than a dozen tables here. Oil landscape paintings are hung on the walls. The waiter, who has coaxed the little hair he has left into a rococo curl on his forehead, recommends the twenty-five franc set menu. They take it. He advises they order house wine from the carafe; white to start, and red for the subsequent courses. Mary Frances realizes later that he knew they were beginners. He knew that the expensive, spectacular wines of the Aux Trois Faisans would be wasted on them at this point.

The waiter with the little curl is called Charles. Over the course of their time in Dijon, he will become their culinary teacher, and this is the evening on which their education begins. They eat the Burgundian dishes; dark, wine-based sauces, richly seasoned, game, and perhaps a soufflé with cherry liquor to round things off. Later, Mary Frances doesn't remember the exact details, but she does recall how they, as newlyweds, ate with such joy and leisure as Charles the waiter tended to them. They felt safe, in good hands, in an enchanted gastronomical world, from which they eventually wandered back to their new home in Dijon, to their little flat, up the crooked, sloping steps.[79]

Their marriage doesn't go well. Eight years later, back home in California, Mary Frances and Al go their separate ways. But the young woman succeeds in making a living by writing about her memories of restaurants like Aux Trois Faisans. She calls herself M. F. K. Fisher. Under this pseudonym, she becomes one of America's most important writers, famous not for novels, dramas or poetry, but her sensual culinary essays. She will go on to write a book about the simultaneously 'dreadful but exciting life' of the oyster.[80] During the Second World War, she supplies Americans with simple recipes that help them to cope with food rationing. She dedicates her entire writing career to the culinary arts.

M. F. K. Fisher is later asked why she devotes her attention to food and not the great literary themes: war, love, power. She answers that the three most basic human needs – for food, security and love – are so 'mixed and mingled and intertwined' that one cannot conceive of one without the other. This is why she writes 'about love and the hunger for it' as well as 'about warmth and the love of it and the hunger for it ... and then the warmth and richness and fine reality of hunger satisfied ... and it is all one'.[81] In Dijon, in 1929, under the aegis of Charles, all of these concepts begin to unite.

*

With his just-licked fingers, the chef picks up the steak. He lays it on the plate. He dips his thumb into the sauce on the plate, licks his thumb, then dunks it once more into the smudge of sauce. The waiter, too, dunks his fingers into the sauce, the same fingers which he regularly runs through his pomade-lacquered hair. If a customer orders a slice of toast, it is a matter of course that the beads of sweat that fall from the waiter's forehead on to the toast will be ignored. If the toast falls, buttered side down, it will be given a quick wipe and served. If a roasted chicken ordered from room service goes flying down the service elevator, three whole floors, and lands in a mixture of discarded breadcrumbs and wastepaper, then it will simply be wiped off, sent back up and presented to the customer. There is dirt everywhere, throughout the building. But the hotel kitchen is the worst. And, of course, the chefs spit in the soup.[82]

Eric Blair's first book betrays all of the hospitality industry's dirty secrets. The literary critic C. Day Lewis recommends that any readers who would like to be able to eat in a restaurant again without experiencing 'acute nausea' avoid pages 107 and 108.[83] But this is also why Blair's book is such a success. Thousands of copies are sold in the first month alone. The *Times Literary Supplement* praises it as a 'vivid picture of an apparently mad world'. The young writer receives fan mail – but also a less than enthusiastic message from a certain Humbert Possenti of Hotel Splendide, London, who has been in the hotel and restaurant business for forty years. Possenti accuses Blair of causing irreparable damage to the world of gastronomy. He declares the book's events to be 'inconceivable'. Eric Blair writes back that his observations would undoubtedly cancel out Humbert Possenti's four decades of life experience. For the first time, he signs his letter with his new name: George Orwell.[84]

*

They simply call him 'the old man'. He's been a waiter for over forty years. He is 'so old', claims Joseph Roth in the *Frankfurter Zeitung* in 1929, that he already has the 'white hair stage behind him', and is now 'well on his way to turning to stone'. The site of his fossilization is the hotel restaurant. He is still able to bow alongside the table. He can tell the young waiter what the guests want. He can guess their desires. He can influence their orders. The ancient waiter and his guests have known each other for decades: 'They all speak', Roth writes, 'the mother tongue of their foregone era.'[85]

Ernest Hemingway's old waiter is not so ossified. He appears in the 1933 short story 'A Clean, Well-Lighted Place'. He argues with his young colleague, who can't accept that a lonely old drinker should not be thrown out. The old waiter tidies up, pulls down the shutters, turns off the light and teaches the young waiter a thing or two about life. He tells him how important a clean, well-illuminated establishment is to people. And at the end of the story, Hemingway's readers plunge into the waiter's inner monologue. He thinks that everything is nothing and that mankind, too, is nothing. Nothing and even more nothing: 'Nada y pues nada.'[86]

Joseph Roth, like Hemingway, also shows his waiter in the face of Nothingness. But he doesn't allow him to become a philosopher. Roth remains the observer, the fossilized waiter his object. He has him speak with a woman of equally advanced years. The lady wears around her 'wrinkled neck' a pearl necklace for which 'her heirs are already waiting'. She has a 'cold, dismissive gaze, the result of a long, rich and carefree life'. She and the waiter extend their hands to one another. According to Roth, class differences no longer matter at their age. They are both preparing 'for the grave', for 'the same earth, the same dust, the same worms'.[87]

*

The extreme right-wing journalist Friedrich Hussong has helped to bury democracy in Germany. As a newspaper columnist, he was one of the leading Nationalist pundits. Now that the Nazis are in power, his career takes a downward turn. In 1934, he is forced to withdraw from political journalism – because he once called Adolf Hitler a 'Wild West politician' and because he's known as an opponent of Hitler's propaganda man Joseph Goebbels.[88]

And so, during the Third Reich, Friedrich Hussong sets to work on a supposedly apolitical text. He becomes a historian and researches the history of German foodways. In 1937, his book *Table of the Centuries* appears. From the Middle Ages to the Rococo, from Biedermeier to the 'Reich and the intermediate Reich', it addresses the various phases of German culinary history. It culminates in the chapter: 'Dream of a German Cuisine'. Hussong aligns himself with the National Socialists' plan to fight the 'lamentable plague of foreigners in German gastronomy'. Eager to participate, he calls for the 'reconstruction of German cuisine'. Much like the early twenty-first-century foodies, he recommends regional and seasonal cooking: 'dishes rooted in the soil' and 'in tune with the seasons'.

This 'Germanization', Hussong finds, should be implemented in restaurants as well. He complains about the 'months of cultural conflict' in the inn where he's a regular. He says he has tried in vain, in this establishment in 'the heart of Berlin', to order not 'ham and eggs' but 'Setzeier mit Schinken'. One needs 'courage and persistence' he claims, to have 'even the smallest glimmer of hope in this respect'. But now the time has come to take a stand, he says. 'Hearty German fare' belongs on 'German menus of the future'. Even Prime Minister Göring, Hussong notes, regards these questions as being 'far from insignificant' when it comes to 'shaping the German fate'.[89]

*

George Orwell's first book sends a shudder down the spine of the gourmet. But for Orwell himself, always a political writer, *Down and Out in Paris and London* is much more than a tale of filth and awful service. His book introduces motifs the author of *1984* will return to again and again: truth and lies, double standards, artificial hierarchies.

The moustache question – waiters without, chefs with, due to superiority over waiters, *plongeurs* without, due to inferiority to waiters – is only the starting point for his analysis. Orwell is familiar with South Asia and its caste system. He discovers one in Parisian gastronomy, too, a finely tuned hierarchy, and he himself is located at the very bottom of it. There's the grimy, dirty kitchen in the Auberge and the pseudo-folklorist interior of the dining room; just a few metres apart, but completely different worlds. There's the waiters' cafeteria in the hotel, where sweating servers with armpit stains gather to eat, the floor below them covered with trampled food, paper and salad leaves. In the gilded dining room, heavy on flowers, the tablecloths are spotless and little cherubs adorn the walls. The two rooms are separated only by a door. And the customers know nothing of what goes on behind it.

Orwell turns his attentions to the survival of those right at the bottom of the system. In the world of gastronomy, he writes, everyone steals, on a daily basis, without even giving it a second thought. Most commonly, the staff steal from the customers. And yet, Orwell also notes, every hotel worker is quick to defend his honour. The cook, for example, doesn't see himself as a servant. Self-confident, never servile, he is certain of his own skills: his powers of recollection, his calm amidst the chaos, his technical abilities. This mindset can be found even further down the caste system. 'Je suis dur,' says a dishwasher, for example, boasting of his toughness. The work means something to the men, it gives them a sense of mas-culinity, however corrupt the system in which it is lived out.[90]

There is one group, however, that doesn't convince Orwell: the waiters. He concludes that his readers should never feel sorry for them. The waiter, he says, has the mentality of a 'snob', because he is constantly in close proximity to the rich, listening to them at their tables, worming his way in with little jokes and smiles. Unlike the chefs and the dishwashers, the waiter identifies himself with the affluent. Indeed, he even delights in his own servility. Orwell watches him move from the dark, dirty area behind the scenes into the public sphere of the dining room, and observes a 'sudden change' in his posture: the waiter suddenly holds his shoulders differently, and glides across the carpet with the ceremonial manner of a priest. One moment, he will be screaming at an apprentice in the kitchen – 'You're not worthy of cleaning the floor in your mother's brothel!' – and in the next he opens the door to the restaurant and glides, 'graceful as a swan', with the plate in his hand over to the customer, a smile on his face. According to Orwell, this provokes feelings of shame in the customer at being served by 'such an aristocrat'.[91]

*

Gerta Pfeffer, a textile designer in a south German weaving mill, sits in an inn with her colleagues. She is enjoying the atmosphere, something she rarely does nowadays. Since the 'Nuremberg Laws' of September 1935, her life has been dominated by fear. She is feeling increasingly isolated, and less and less willing to talk to people in public. She is afraid that either someone could start a rumour about her for being a Jew, or that someone else could come to harm through having contact with her. While other young people go dancing, she spends most of her time alone. Tonight, though, here in this restaurant and in the company of her colleagues, Gerta Pfeffer is feeling cheerful again. Which prompts the diners at the next table to tell the innkeepers that if they see the Jewess laugh one more time they'll throw her out on the street.[92]

*

George Orwell is going down below with the miners. He observes their bodies, their broad shoulders, their narrow and lithe hips, their wiry legs. Not an ounce of fat to be seen. He is amazed by their work, their dexterity below ground. He marvels at the energy produced by the coalmines, without which nothing in the world could function.

In his book *The Road to Wigan Pier*, Orwell describes the working-class world of 1937. He contemplates the social situation in England, the needs of the working and middle classes, and ends the book on an optimistic note. Joining forces with these men – in his opinion – could enable a socialist party to be successful in England.

Now the lessons he learned during his time as a dishwasher in the restaurant kitchen become even more tangible. What he observed in Parisian restaurants leads him to question whether elite gastronomy should even exist. Why do kitchen workers have to slave away? Does it serve civilization in any form or manner? Orwell thinks not. To him, luxury consumerism serves only one purpose: it feeds the upper classes' fear of the lower classes. There is nothing to justify fancy restaurants or hotels, and all they offer is shabby imitation. Any employment in these places contributes to the 'shams which are supposed to represent luxury'. The only person who profits is the owner of the establishment in question, buying himself a 'striped villa in Deauville'.[93]

The miners, with their powerful shoulders, represent a vision of a future in which class differences have dissolved. Their strength, Orwell hopes, could even pull the underprivileged up with the coal. The waiters, by contrast, sometimes graceful like swans, sometimes ceremonial like priests, and always ready with a smile at the tables of the rich: they embody the system that George Orwell attacks.

*

Sitting on his cart, behind the horse, the cattle trader makes his way through the Rhön. It is a land in the heart of Germany, of forests and meadows, mountains and valleys. He was born here, north-east of the Wasserkuppe mountain, where his family has lived for generations. His cart rolls down into the Ulstergrund, to Hilders, to Baten, then uphill to Brand. Above him, on the Tannenfels, the ruin of Eberstein Castle bears witness to thirteenth-century feuds. In the inn at Brand, he sees proprietor Gensler standing by the window. They have always been good friends. And so the cattle trader, David Grünspecht is his name, stops the cart and climbs down from the coach box. He recently received his immigration papers for the United States, and he wants to drink one last cognac with Gensler.

Inside the almost empty inn, he and Gensler stand at the bar. A stranger, sitting alone at a table, addresses them. He uses an insult which has become very popular in German everyday life of late, and which refers to the supposed smell of Jews. The stranger says: 'It stinks of garlic in here all of a sudden.' Grünspecht and Gensler ignore him. But the man persists: 'Herr Innkeeper, is there a garlic field near here? The stench is unbearable.'[94]

*

In 1938, Joseph Wechsberg is warning people off American food. Off sandwiches ('two slabs of air bread'), off 'half raw and indigestible steaks', off 'conserves devoid of nutritional value'.[95] He advises against having one's lunch in 'one minute restaurants' and complains about American women, who, in his opinion, 'have no sense of congeniality, friendship or feeling' and who want to be taken out not to one establishment, but to five in a row, where, according to Wechsberg, one is always served up 'the same bellowing music, the same whiskey and the same check'.[96]

Nonetheless, Joseph Wechsberg, a Jewish lawyer from Moravian Ostrava, has no plans to return to Europe. He and his wife came to the USA in 1938 with a delegation from the Czechoslovakian government, and have been there ever since.[97] He plans to bring over as many refugees as possible,

sets about collecting tips on immigration, and in 1939 publishes the guidebook *Visa for America*. Wechsberg writes for
those who want to 'turn their back on Europe as quickly as
possible'. He explains everything they need to know about
affidavits, immigration quotas and visa categories.

Wechsberg also states how pointless it is to take 'European
ideas' along to the United States. He explicitly warns his coun-
trymen against trying to sell smoked meats in America: there
are no profits to be made from such wares in the land of 'juice
restaurants and oyster bars and steakhouses'. And it would
be an equally bad idea, Wechsberg states, to open a Viennese-
style *Kaffeehaus* in a mid-sized American town filled with
'petrol fumes, small-town puritanism, drugstores and local
boosterism'. All European-born concepts, by no means limited
to smoked meats and coffee houses, are 'sentenced to death',
Wechsberg warns, in the United States. Americans are 'happy
that there are 5,000 kilometres of water between Europe and
America'. Their only regret, according to Wechsberg, is 'that
there aren't 50,000'.[98]

*

On the site of a former landfill in Queens, a French restaurant opens its doors. It is 1939. The French government has
employed chefs from the very best establishments in Paris. On
the Atlantic steamer *Normandie*, they have crossed around
5,000 kilometres of water in order to bring their concept of
pleasure to the Americans. The name of this gourmet restaurant is Le Pavillon de France, and it is the French contribution
to the 1939 World's Fair, which takes place on the boggy site of
Flushing Meadows, New York. The exhibition celebrates the
idea of a peaceful, progress-orientated world for the last time
before the outbreak of the Second World War. The Lagoon

of Nations sparkles in the sun. General Motors presents the optimistically utopian Futurama. In front of the Soviet pavilion, a heroic worker stretches up into the heights. In the French pavilion, they cook.

On 9 May 1939, the French ambassador and three hundred guests arrive for the first celebratory meal. The chefs present a ten-course menu, which commences with a 'Double Consommé de Vieur' and progresses via the 'Homard Pavillon de France' to the 'Noisette de Prés-Salé Ambassadrice'. To finish, there are 'Frivolités Parisiennes'. A total of 18,401 meals are served in the first month, 26,510 in the second. Overall, 136,000 guests will dine at Flushing Meadows.

*

He is forty-two years old, almost forty-three, when he travels to Paris. He has tea in Palais Rothschild. Then he visits an exhibition of Flemish textiles. 'Simply wonderful. I am transfixed', he notes in his journal. He extols the 'old magic of this wonderful city', now 'pulsating with life' once more. He wanders through the streets and buys 'charming toys' for his children. In the evenings, he eats in a restaurant in Rue Royale, just a few steps away from Jardin des Tuileries: Maxim's. It is, he declares, 'a splendid life'.[99]

The traveller in question is Joseph Goebbels. It is October 1940, and he is visiting German-occupied Paris. In his journals from these years, Goebbels often writes about the establishments he has dined in. Following the Austrian Anschluss, after visiting Hitler's childhood home (where Goebbels breathes in the air so deeply and his mood becomes 'great and joyful'), he stops off to eat in the Weisses Rössl at Wolfgangsee.[100] After the anti-Jewish pogroms across Germany in November 1938, he notes in his journal that he gave his report to Adolf Hitler in the leader's favourite establishment, Osteria Bavaria, one of the first Italian restaurants in Munich. 'He is in agreement with everything,' Goebbels writes in summary of their conversation over dinner. 'The mission went flawlessly. Seventeen casualties. But no German property has been damaged.'[101]

In February 1943, Goebbels will coin the expression 'total war'. At the restaurant Maxim's, however, he likes the fact that there is no trace of the war. He gets on swimmingly with his table companion. 'Göring is marvellous,' Goebbels notes after leaving the restaurant, back at his hotel. 'He's such an endearing fellow.'

The next day, he has representatives of the Luftwaffe outline the plan for the bombardment of England, which is 'to be carried out with German efficiency'. The plan impresses him. (A few days later he will write the following lines in his diary: 'Excellent reports from London. It's hell on earth there.') He rants about the Francophilia rife amongst diplomats in the German Embassy in the French capital: It's enough to 'make one want to vomit.' Then he spends his last Parisian evening 'in a little establishment where French chansons are sung'. And he finds the restaurant 'pleasant and charming'. As if catching himself with some forbidden thought, he immediately adds a note that Paris represents 'a great danger', in particular for 'apolitical Germans'. Then he flies back to Berlin.[102]

*

After the World's Fair has come to a close, the Pavillon de France moves – but not back to Paris. The chefs and waiters are more taken with the idea of staying in the United States than returning to their Nazi-occupied home town. On 15 October 1941, Le Pavillon opens as a gourmet restaurant on 55th Street, just a few steps away from Fifth Avenue. It quickly becomes one of the most sophisticated addresses in Manhattan. Caviar is served, as well as 'Sole Bonne Femme' and 'Poulet Braisé au Champagne'. The prices are extremely high. But VIP guests can count on receiving free champagne and other forms of special treatment. The Pavillon becomes the Kennedys' favourite restaurant. It is a little piece of France in midtown Manhattan. The menus describe the dishes on offer in French, without any translation into English. And the chefs' hats from Le Pavillon are sent back to the Old World again and again. French nuns look after them. They clean and press the caps as they do their own robes.[103]

*

Jean-Paul Sartre is living in German-occupied Paris and has issues with the service. They are similar to the difficulties George Orwell experienced. Sartre notes that the waiter's movement is 'quick and forward, a little too precise, a little too rapid', that he approaches the patrons with a 'step a little too quick', and 'bends forward a little too eagerly'. This impression is intensified further, he says, by the waiter's voice and his eyes; the latter 'express an interest a little too solicitous for the order of the customer'.[104]

These thoughts arise when Sartre has just returned to Paris after his time as a German prisoner of war. It is a humbling phase in his life. He tries to build up a resistance group. But the risk of paying for its actions with his life seems too great. So he begins to act politically through his writing instead.[105] In the monumental text he is working on, *Being and Nothingness*, he is developing a philosophy of freedom. In order to illustrate the concept, Sartre describes a restaurant to the reader. The sign 'Entry forbidden to Jews' or – bitter irony – the plaque 'Jewish restaurant, access forbidden to Aryans', doesn't stand in the way of the customer's personal freedom, claims Sartre. The way in which someone reacts to the sign in front of the establishment, whether they ignore it or obey it, is dependent only on the 'weight' which they themselves attribute to the ban.[106]

As concrete as this example may be, Sartre's thinking is abstract, rather than a recommendation of how to act. The philosopher is well aware that any rebellious defiance of the rules can have fatal consequences in occupied Paris. In stark contrast to this radical concept for freedom, Sartre sees in the restaurant not only prohibition signs to be courageously ignored, but also a waiter who, far from projecting defiance and freedom, imitates 'the inflexible stiffness of some kind of automaton' even in his servile manner of walking. He seems as mechanical as he is theatrical. The waiter, Sartre concludes, embodies inauthenticity and lack of freedom.[107]

*

The German bombing attacks are inflicting more and more damage on English cities. Water, electricity and gas lines have been hit. A period of food shortages begins, one which will continue in Great Britain until long after the war has ended. In the autumn of 1940, the first feeding stations are set up in London, offering cheap, hot meals from mobile kitchens. These are often housed in evacuated schools, partly because this means that otherwise unoccupied home economics teachers can run them. The concept is successful: 139 kitchens produce 80,000 meals per week. In November 1940, the project is to be expanded to other major English cities: Birmingham, Manchester, Liverpool and others. The working title of the project has been decided upon: the feeding stations are to be called 'Community Kitchens'.

Winston Churchill isn't so keen. The concept itself certainly conforms to what he had in mind. But the Conservative prime minister doesn't like words such as 'community' and 'communal'; to him, they reek of communism and workhouses. The future winner of the Nobel Prize for Literature searches for a term which will reassure people that they'll receive a good meal. Once he finds it – 'British Restaurants' – the name sticks, and the kitchens go on to feed around half a million British people through the worst periods of the Second World War. Future historians will regard their role in the provision of nourishment as marginal. But they also acknowledge one significant consequence: the 'British Restaurants' accustom a good number of otherwise home-loving English people to take the risk of eating out.[108]

*

The role played by the waiter in Jean-Paul Sartre's edifice of ideas is far from insignificant. He represents what the philosopher calls 'bad faith'. A person who has succumbed to this is deceiving himself. He hovers between transcendence and facticity, not knowing the difference between these two modes of existence. For Sartre, the 'first act' of 'bad faith' is a flight from the things one cannot escape.[109] And the waiter, too quick, too automated, too servile, does exactly that. He escapes into the game of being a waiter. He may of course reflect on the fact that he has to get up at five o'clock in the morning, that he is supposed to sweep the floor before the restaurant opens, that he has to get the coffee pot going, that he has a right to the tips and the right to belong to a union. But he is part of the fiction of the waiter and has lost the sense of how to be free and responsible for himself.[110]

*

In June 1944, William Foote Whyte comes to Chicago to research restaurants. Unlike Frances Donovan, the outsider, Whyte is one of the most established sociologists of his time. In his book *Street Corner Society*, he investigated an Italian neighbourhood of Boston and composed a groundbreaking work of urban sociology: up close and personal to the informants whose world he describes in the greatest of detail. Now Whyte holds a research post for organizational sociology at the University of Chicago. He is leading a collaborative project with the National Restaurant Association of the United States.

William Foote Whyte does not look for a job as a waiter; he is not able to. A short while before, he contracted polio during a stay in Oklahoma. For the rest of his life, he will be reliant on a walking stick, and later on crutches. But he doesn't need to enter the service industry personally in order to carry out his research; he has plenty of staff at his disposal for that. One of Whyte's assistants, for example, is to contribute observations from an establishment called Harding's to the project. The up-and-coming researcher follows in Frances Donovan's footsteps, claiming to be a waitress in search of a job. And at Harding's, her future boss assures her: 'I think you will enjoy working here – we don't employ any Jews or negroes.'

*

Frances Donovan is feared by the children at her school. As vice-principal at Calamut High School, she is responsible for disciplinary problems, and takes her job very seriously. Some pupils appreciate her, and credit her for having inspired and encouraged them to pursue academic careers. But many are afraid of her.

Like the waitress, the teacher, too, has an inner life which isn't publicly discernible. Donovan, for example, has not lost her interest in writing. She is now working on short stories. She still lives in the middle of the city, but the smog, the cacophony of the traffic, and the views of concrete walls are starting to bother her. She prepares for her retirement and plans to leave Chicago. By May 1945, she will be ready.

*

Crying waitresses play a key role in William Foote Whyte's study of the restaurant. He depicts the 'great American drama of food, hospitality and personal service' which plays out there every day. And he shows that the relationship between managers and their subordinates is, in most establishments, a very tense one. Hardly any effort is put into human relationships. And this is why the waitresses' tears, nervous breakdowns and confidence crises are part of day-to-day life. Whyte has a solution at the ready: with practised 'teamwork' and 'skilful supervision', the sensitive equilibrium of the restaurant can be maintained. Then the waitresses will hardly ever cry. The key factor here is the balance of a 'sensitive machine', according to Whyte – and it remains unclear who or what this machine is: the gastronomy industry or the serving staff themselves.[111]

Frances the waitress doesn't cry. She is new in Chicago, from a small town in the Midwest. In the restaurant she immediately exudes a confident air, showing courage and initiative. The stress of the lunch service drives her good friend Mary to hysterical breakdowns in the staff toilet. Frances, in contrast, stays strong.[112]

She is not the same Frances who once researched waitresses in Chicago in 1917. Frances Donovan, pioneer in restaurant research, participant observer in a waitress's apron, doesn't appear in William Foote Whyte's great study: not in the text, not in the references, and not in the acknowledgements. Donovan has left Chicago. Since May of 1945, she has been living in Eureka Springs in the state of Arkansas. There, in her early sixties, she will begin her next research project: a micro-sociological study of her new home town.[113]

2

Postwar Hunger

J ames Baldwin is going to throw a jug of water at a waitress. What he really wants to do is strangle her. Baldwin grew up in Harlem, the heart of African American culture. He is the son of a Baptist preacher, and as a teenager he was already leading his own church services. In Harlem he is renowned for his sharp mind and rhetorical skills. Now, however, in the year 1942, he finds himself on the other side of the Hudson, in New Jersey. He is working in an arms factory. Geographically speaking, he's not far from home. But many of his colleagues here, both black and white, come from strictly segregated Southern states. And so the codes of the South have been brought to New Jersey.

It takes Baldwin a while to figure this out. On three separate occasions, he visits the same self-service restaurant, stands at the counter with white colleagues his age, orders and is confused as to why it takes so long for him to receive his hamburger and coffee. On the fourth visit, he realizes that he wasn't actually served at all on the previous three visits. Instead, unaware, he had consumed another customer's hamburger and coffee. In this establishment meals and drinks are not served to black customers. Segregation reigns everywhere – including bars, bowling lanes and apartment buildings – and again and again James Baldwin comes up against these unwritten rules. He stands out, is laughed at, shouted at. Eventually, he loses his job.

On his last evening in New Jersey, he makes plans with a white friend. They go to the cinema to watch *This Land is Mine*, a film about the German occupation of France. After the movie, they go for something to eat. The restaurant is called American Diner. 'What do you want?' asks the man at the counter. 'We want a hamburger and a cup of coffee,' Baldwin retorts. 'What do you think we want?' But that wasn't the question.[1]

*

Simon Wiesenthal, an architect, survives his time in the ghetto. He narrowly escapes being shot. He makes attempts at suicide. He survives a death march to Buchenwald and a transport to Mauthausen. Now, in the spring of 1945, he is in the concentration camp's so-called death block, and he is starving. He is 1.80 metres and weighs less than 50 kilos. The liberation is imminent and American planes are flying over the camp. But day after day in the block, the prisoners continue to die.

Wiesenthal gets into conversation with a Polish food porter: Eduard Staniszewski. They know each other from Posen. Staniszewski wants to open a new gastronomic venture after the end of the war, and asks Wiesenthal to draw up some architectural plans for him. He brings him pencils and paper. Wiesenthal sets to work. He makes a variety of sketches for the establishment, enough for an entire book. He even draws the waitresses' uniforms. In the death block, the prisoners are dying. Their daily food ration consists of two hundred calories. Eduard Staniszewski brings Wiesenthal extra bread in exchange for his ideas. They speak about what shape the tables should be. They discuss carpets and colours.

Even after the liberation of Mauthausen, thousands of prisoners go on to die of malnourishment. Eduard Staniszewski will keep Wiesenthal's sketches safely tucked away for many decades. The establishment they planned never opens. But Simon Wiesenthal survives.[2]

*

Wolfram Siebeck is seventeen and hungry. He lives in Bochum, a coal and steel town in the Ruhr Valley. In the war he was a Flakhelfer, then, briefly, a soldier. He had signed up to the Wehrmacht voluntarily. In the spring of 1945, he manned an anti-aircraft post on the Oder river, then headed west, giving Berlin a wide berth. He has seen dead concentration-camp internees lying in ditches at the side of the roads. In May 1945, he ended up in a prisoner-of-war camp. With hardly anything to eat. Soon after, he was transferred to another camp. He went hungry there too, for months on end, and through all this he constantly played cards. After being discharged he spent time in the Black Forest, where farmers' wives fattened him up with never-ending quantities of food. The hunger passed. Now he is back home in Bochum, where the steel mills have been destroyed by the war. And the hunger is back.[3]

In 1945 and 1946, adult Germans consume an average of 1,412 calories per day, though the official ration allows just 860 calories.[4] Some of Wolfram's older relatives have already died of malnourishment. Hoping to stave off his family's hunger, he sets off to see a card-playing contact from the prisoner-of-war camp, a farmer living one hour to the north. But he is not the only one who has had this idea; he arrives to find his camp buddies already there. Now they are competing for ham, butter and potatoes.

The boy from the Ruhr Valley turns up at the farm again and again. Often he has nothing he can exchange, not even for some grains or some windfall fruit. Black beetles scrabble around inside a sack of pearl barley he has managed to scavenge. He carefully picks them out.[5]

*

American journalists are out and about in postwar Paris. They discover a new generation of French intellectuals who spend their days in cafés and restaurants. A reporter from *Time* magazine spots Jean-Paul Sartre in Café de Flore and claims that Sartre can always be found there, writing and preaching. The writer's colleague, from *Life* magazine, heads to the same establishment and sees Sartre receiving visitors, having business meetings, giving interviews. The philosopher sleeps in a hotel room, according to a *New York Times* journalist, and lives at the table of this café. American reporters are so interested in French thinkers and their favourite establishments that, in December 1946, a *Time* reporter even asks a waiter from Café de Flore for his take on Existentialism. The waiter, whose name is Pascal, declares himself to be in full agreement with Sartre's ideas.

The American fascination with philosophers who dine out is not entirely coincidental. During the postwar period in the United States, the role of the intellectual is redefined. Influential thinkers no longer see themselves as critical outsiders, but as vital middle-class patriots. They are the driving forces of a new, efficient society which now finds itself in the midst of the Cold War. In contrast, Jean-Paul Sartre and Simone de Beauvoir appear as barely credible hedonists, their left-wing pessimism no more than a pose.

To highlight the obvious contradictions of European intellectualism, the American media eagerly emphasize the luxurious hedonism of Sartre and de Beauvoir's Parisian café lifestyle. They report on 'succulent dinners, topped by excellent vintages and rounded off by age-ripened liqueurs', and on their trips to nightclubs, where the pessimistic intellectuals dance into the early hours of the morning.[6]

*

In the American Diner, Baldwin and his friend are turned away with the words: 'We don't serve negroes here.' The usual response. Baldwin is struck by the irony of the restaurant's name and the way it treats Americans like him. At first he stays calm. But back on the busy street, he is gripped by rage. He feels as though everyone around him is white, as if they're all closing in on him, wanting to attack him. He walks on as though in a trance, hears the voice of his white friend behind him, speeds up, runs and feels his anger growing stronger. He reaches an elegant, sparkling, huge restaurant. He knows very well that they will never serve him here. But he doesn't care. He goes in and sits at the first free table he sees. The waitress appears. She is white. Baldwin sees the fear in her widened eyes, and that makes him even angrier. He wants to give her a reason for her fear.

'We don't serve negroes here,' she says. Her tone isn't hostile, it's apologetic, and genuinely afraid. Baldwin longs to feel her neck between his hands, to strangle her. He acts as though he hasn't understood; he wants her to come closer, so he can attack her. She takes just a small step in his direction. Then she says her rehearsed line one more time. 'We don't serve negroes here.'[7]

*

Joseph Wechsberg's father fell in the First World War. His mother was murdered in Auschwitz. He survived. And now he is writing about the fascinating variety of boiled beef on offer in the restaurant of the Viennese hotel Meissl & Schadn. The following delicacies are served there, up on the first floor: Mittleres Kügerl, Dünnes Kügerl, Dickes Kügerl, Weisses Scherzl, Schwarzes Scherzl, Tafelspitz, Tafeldeckel, Schulterschwanz, Schulterscherzl, Hieferschwanzl, Bröselfleisch, Ausgelöstes, Brustkern, Brustfleisch, Kavalierspitz and Kruspelspitz. And more besides. Even 'fellow Austrians from the dark, Alpine hinterlands of Salzburg and Tyrol rarely knew the fine points of distinction between, say, Tafelspitz, Schwarzes Scherzl and Hieferschwanzl – all referred to in America as brisket or plate of beef – or between the various Kügerls,' writes Wechsberg. In fact, the terminology 'was bound to stump anybody who had not spent the first half of his adult life within the city limits of Vienna'. None of the guests would dream of ordering 'boiled beef' here, just as no customer at Tiffany's would ever just ask for a 'stone'. Everyone knows about the thirty-two different cuts and the four specific quality levels. Diners here consider themselves to be members of a very exclusive club. And even the cattle are part of it: they are reared on the site of a sugar refinery in a village north of Vienna and fed with sugar-beet purée. This sets the quality of their meat apart from the rest.

Whether every customer really does belong to the club is not clear in Meissl & Schadn. The head waiter, Heinrich, greets the customers on the first floor. The gradient of his bow indicates Heinrich's assessment of each customer's social standing. For the nouveau riche, he makes a half bow. The full bow is only performed after twenty-five to thirty years of loyal custom. A commis chef brings the meat out on a silver platter, concealed beneath the lid. A piccolo serves the garnishes: pickled horseradish, apple horseradish, horseradish cream, cabbage, spinach, potatoes, gherkins. A waiter lifts the lid, presents the meat to the customer, then places it on to a hot plate. Then the waiter looks at the head waiter, and the customer looks at the head waiter, and the head waiter looks at the meat, through almost-closed eyelids, then nods lightly, very lightly, towards the waiter, towards the customer. Only then can the customer eat. Or can he? No, he can't. Not any more.

In March 1945, an American bomb hit the Meissl & Schadn building. Later, the Russian liberating forces threw explosives into the half-destroyed house. Meissl & Schadn is history. Joseph Wechsberg's readers only discover this at the end of his travel report on postwar Austria. Viennese cattle are no longer eating puréed sugar beet. Their meat is now dry and tough. Viennese chefs no longer know how to cut a rump (lengthways along the foremost part, diagonally towards the end of the flesh triangle). Viennese waiters are only interested in tips, and no longer in their customers' palates. This is how Joseph Wechsberg, once of Moravian Ostrava, now of New York City, assesses the situation after a visit to the former capital of cooked beef.[8]

*

There is another kind of hunger: the intellectual kind. In his war-ravaged home town Wolfram Siebeck becomes a voracious regular at a private lending library. He devours the books, everything from Arthur Conan Doyle to Dostoyevsky and Canetti, and reads literary journals like *Die Frankfurter Hefte* and *Die Gegenwart*, along with anything else he can get his hands on. The reading distracts him from his ever-present hunger. But that is as far as his ambition goes: he is an individualist, a slacker, a drifter. He doesn't go back to school because there they act as though the war never happened. He shirks out of rubble clean-up operations. He is unemployed. Sometimes, when forced to, he does some garden work at a cemetery in Bochum. Sometimes he hires himself out as a sign painter. He enjoys hanging around in bars. Anything in any way connected to the common good or authority has become suspect to him following his experiences during the war.

In July 1948, when he is twenty years old, he finds a job that means something to him: as an illustrator for the *Westdeutsche Allgemeine Zeitung*. When he goes in to deliver his illustrations, he drinks bad wine with the editors. Back at home, in the flat he shares with his mother and grandmother, there is now enough to eat. The monetary reform changed everything: now there's buttercream cake, accompanied by home-made egg liqueur. It's thick, syrupy, viscous, and he later remembers how he would lick it out of the glass in ecstasy. These are the recollections of Wolfram Siebeck, the renowned German writer and food critic.[9]

*

James Baldwin gets up from his chair. He picks up the half-full jug of water from the table. He hurls it at the waitress. She ducks. The jug smashes against the mirror behind the counter. Mouths drop open across the restaurant, customers jump to their feet. Then Baldwin's rage turns to fear. He runs to the door, is grabbed by a man who punches him in the face, kicks him. Baldwin tears himself free, runs out on to the street, stumbles into his white friend and keeps running, while the friend throws the pursuers and police off his trail.

Baldwin will live through this moment again and again. He will write about it, thirteen years later, in 'Notes of a Native Son', one of his masterful essays addressing life in a country shaped by racist ideas. The world is no longer white and will never be white again. This is the idea which drives Baldwin's work. What he learns from the restaurants of New Jersey is that hate will always destroy the person who feels it.[10]

*

Jacques, thirteen years old, is told to fetch the chicken deboning machine. The Hôtel de France has it. And it's needed urgently. It is late summer, in the year 1948. Jacques has been a cooking apprentice in the restaurant of the Grand Hôtel de l'Europe for just two weeks. And now this important task. He hurries, running more than walking, across to the far side of Bourg-en-Bresse, where the head chef is already waiting for him, shaking his head sympathetically, to inform him that his colleague at L'Escargot is in possession of the machine. And so Jacques hastens on, for another two kilometres or more, only to find another regretful head chef, who informs him that the restaurant of Hôtel Terminus now has it. He keeps running, another head chef: no, the chicken-deboning machine is in the kitchen of L'Escargot after all. Once more he runs through the streets of Bourg-en-Bresse and, finally, redemption: at L'Escargot, the chef presses a large, sealed linen sack into his hands. Thank God – the desperately needed chicken-deboning machine, strangely heavy, is his at last. Jacques runs back, as quickly as he can. Carefully, carefully, the machine mustn't get damaged, but quickly nonetheless, for it is needed so urgently. Exhausted, Jacques Pépin, who half a century later will be one of the most famous television chefs in the United States, veers into Rue Bichat. He is back at last, at his workplace,

the Grand Hôtel de l'Europe. Where his superiors, his fellow
apprentices, the waitresses are waiting for him. Where he opens
the linen sack to find no chicken deboning machine, but two
large blocks of cement. Immense laughter. Immense shame.
Now he is one of them.[11]

*

A strict hierarchy reigns in this hotel. Everyone knows who
runs things and who takes the reservations. It is also clear who
carries the luggage, shines the shoes and empties the guests'
bedpans. The hotel is situated on Unst, one of the Shetland
Islands and the most northerly inhabited island of Great
Britain. It is the early 1950s. There is a world of difference, in
social terms, between the tray-carrying girls who serve in the
hotel restaurant and the managers, who belong to the middle
class. That, at least, is what the guests think.

In the kitchen, inside which no guest ever steps foot, it's a
different scene. When everyone eats together here, you hardly
see any difference between the business manager right at the
top of the hierarchy and the fourteen-year-old dishwasher
right at the bottom. They all call each other by their first
names, gossip, hold their cutlery in their fists, peel potatoes,
drink tea out of cups without using saucers, eat their main
meal from the bowl which they previously spooned their soup
out of. Damp socks are hung out to dry over the hearth. The
kitchen boys spit into the coal bucket. Women put their feet up.
The manager keeps his hat on. They can be themselves here.

And yet there is an outsider watching them. He is in his
late twenties, an American agricultural technician. Or at least
that's what he says. Some people on Unst think he's a spy.
And they are right not to trust him. Because in truth Erving
Goffmann isn't a US citizen, as he claims, but a Canadian by

birth. And his interest lies not in farming technology, but in how people behave in daily life. He is a doctoral student at the University of Chicago, at the world-famous sociology department. He has travelled to Unst to conduct research for his thesis. It will develop into one of the most influential sociology books of the twentieth century: *The Presentation of Self in Everyday Life*.

The kitchen and the public dining room are ideal territory for Goffman's theories. From his observations here, he develops the theory of location-specific self-representation: clearly defined spaces in which people represent themselves in clearly defined ways. Everyone does this, Goffman shows, not just opportunists. People strive to employ appropriate techniques in social interactions. This is 'impression management', and it is also the reason why Erving Goffman keeps looking at the door between the hotel restaurant and the kitchen. It separates one stage from the other, the 'front', from the 'back'. The waitresses would prefer the door to be kept open: because they carry heavy trays, because they need to watch the customers, because they themselves are constantly being watched anyhow; they are part of the 'front'. The managers want the door to be kept closed. They need the situation to be clearly defined – as authorities in 'front' who decide how things are done, as chatting eaters out 'back' in the kitchen, next to spitting dishwasher boys, beneath damp socks on the hearth. Every day, the door between the dining room and kitchen is either opened angrily by someone (a waitress) or closed angrily by someone else (a manager). And then the pseudo-American agricultural technician actually does have a technical idea. He recommends they put a small glass window in the door, in order to make restaurant life easier.[12]

*

The apprentice Jacques Pépin learns to cook not through words, but through osmosis. Recipes don't matter. In the kitchen of the Grand Hôtel de l'Europe, he sharpens his senses. He learns how to tell whether meat is cooked just by pressing it with his finger. His ears help him assess the freshness of an apple through its crunch and of a stalk of asparagus by the sound of its snap. When the chicken sings in the oven, as they say here, it's almost done, because the juices will now run clear. He learns the respective scents of pears, oranges, tomatoes, melons, when they have reached just the right degree of ripeness.

After the apprenticeship, he leaves Bourg-en-Bresse for Paris. He works in Le Maxéville on Boulevard Montmartre, where a women's string orchestra provides acoustic accompaniment to the dining. The cooking there is too simple for him. They put together routine bistro meals, like sauerkraut with meat, like onion soup. He keeps looking. He cooks in Le Meurice, the favourite haunt of German generals during the Occupation. Here, the chef gives his orders through a megaphone. Pépin is responsible for vegetables and soup. Soon he gets bored again. He finds a new position at La Rotonde, a brasserie in Montparnasse. One day, the waiter calls him to the dividing door between the kitchen and the dining room and points out a customer to him. This man is sitting alone at the table, wearing an undertaker's suit, with thick glasses and tangled hair, an ugly man who makes no attempt not to appear so, bowing his torso right over the plate as he eats, reading and chewing at the same time: Jean-Paul Sartre, a regular. The head chef at La Rotonde is probably the last man in Paris who still has a Hitler moustache. After numerous confrontations with him, Jacques hands in his notice.

He finally finds his professional home in La Plaza Athénée. Forty-eight cooks work here, rotating between the stations in the classic French brigade system. They are generalists, competent in every area of the kitchen. Each cook has learnt every handgrip at every station. They have five weeks of holiday per year, a private nurse at their disposal and a private library filled with literary and philosophical works. They have their own canoe on the River Seine, and their own football and basketball teams. They are spoilt. But they are never creative or individualist, not ever. There is no space for self-expression in this kitchen. Everything is carried out exactly as the unwritten rules of the house dictate. The customer should never be able to notice which individual has prepared a specific dish. Jacques Pépin feels at home in this system.[13]

*

In 1952, the restaurant in Würzburg's Elefantengasse gets new leaseholders. She, Janina Schmitt, is a ballet dancer. He, Nicola di Camillo, is an experienced clothes salesman who has worked as a front desk manager at an American armed forces' club. Di Camillo knows what GIs like to eat, and he wants to open a 'Ristorante Pizzeria' for them. An Italian friend takes charge of the kitchen.

The owner isn't overly enthusiastic and demands that the traditional German name of the restaurant be maintained. The leaseholders see things differently. They want something Italian. A compromise is eventually found: the restaurant is now called Uffenheimer Braustüberl: Le Sabbie di Capri. It opens on 24 March 1952. It is the first German pizzeria.

Germans rarely come to the restaurant. Many are unable to afford it in these postwar years. Others have misgivings about the exotic menu. American soldiers are Schmitt and di Camillo's primary clientele. They are served spaghetti with meatballs, which is both a speciality from Abruzzo, where di Camillo comes from, and an American staple.[14]

Twenty years later, German pizzerias will turn over hundreds of millions of Deutschmarks a year. Gastronomy once regarded as 'foreign' will change the face of the Federal Republic. Italian restaurants will represent new forms of zest for life, of romanticism, as German towns import *italianità*. The food, waiters and interior design bring a whole new atmosphere of freedom and sensuality to Germany. The Italian migrants become 'role models', writes the historian Maren Möhring six decades after the renovation of the Uffenheimer Braustüberl. Their establishments serve as 'sites of mass-cultural adaptation to the foreign' and as institutions of 'civil interaction' with 'the other'. The Federal Republic of Germany limits the political participation of even long-term migrants. The newcomers shape society with their restaurants instead.[15]

Soon the Franconians have more money and fewer misgivings. The leaseholders of the Uffenheimer Braustüberl are so successful that the German part of the name is allowed to disappear. The restaurant is now simply called Capri. Two years later, Schmitt and di Camillo go on holiday to Italy for the first time. After their return, they renovate the restaurant in the style of the Blue Grotto. With the aid of a great deal of plaster, the cellar is designed to look like the famous cave, while the bar takes on the form of a gondola. Romantically inclined Würzberg residents meet here for rendezvous. In 1961, the German trade magazine *Die Küche* prophesies that 'the pizza will [...] find friends here'.[16]

*

Craig Claiborne, PR man for Fluffo margarine, is sitting with a woman at a bad table in the New York restaurant the Colony. He has just ordered a bottle of Puligny-Montrachet from the arrogant sommelier. They gave him this small table right in the restaurant's no-man's-land, because he, Craig Claiborne, is a nobody. At least for now, in the year 1956. He comes from Mississippi, was a soldier in the Second World War and the Korean War, has a degree in journalism, trained at the world-famous hotel school in Lausanne and harbours dreams of a glamorous job with a big-city newspaper. So far, however, he has had little success. Fluffo, with its intense yellow pigment, resembles butter only in terms of colour, but Claiborne is writing a cookery book encouraging Americans to bake with it. He even recommends Fluffo for wedding cakes. And now he is taking this lady, a magazine editor, out for dinner at the Colony. He wants her to take an interest in Fluffo – hopefully, one day, she'll include a Fluffo-based recipe in her magazine.

The sommelier returns to the table. He is an extremely serious, gaunt man, who serves Claiborne with a robot-like charm. In New York at this time, French restaurants are bastions of snobbishness. The sommelier pours a few drops of the supposed Puligny-Montrachet into Claiborne's glass. Out of the corner of his eye, Claiborne spots the name Chassagne on the bottle, but he keeps that to himself. He put the glass up to his nose and breathes in deeply, takes a sip, lets the wine circulate in his mouth, swallows. He says: This is very strange, but the wine tastes like Chassagne-Montrachet. But, *Monsieur*, replies the waiter, this is most definitely Puligny-Montrachet, not Chassagne-Montrachet, vineyards which are admittedly very close to one another in Burgundy, but nonetheless entirely different. Craig Claiborne expresses further doubt. He asks to see the bottle. And from that moment on, he is no longer a nobody, at least not in the Colony, where the manager himself wants to meet the man with such an unbelievably fine-tuned wine palate. And he never again seats Craig at a bad table when he's there winning friends for Fluffo.[17]

*

Gael Greene also finds herself unsure of what to do with her life in the year 1956. She is twenty-one and has just left college. She, too, wants to make it as a journalist. Right now she is at home in Detroit, Michigan, where she works for United Press International. One thing is keeping her spirits up: Elvis Presley is coming to town. He's scheduled to give two open-air concerts. And Gael Greene, a big fan, writes to Colonel Parker, Elvis's manager, saying she wants to spend the day with Elvis so she can write an article about it for UPI. The idea is inspired. But all she receives back is a mimeographed invitation to the official press conference.

Nonetheless, she ends up going to bed with Elvis. Because she flirts with a security guard. Because she stands out in the press conference amidst the sea of male reporters. Because Elvis looks at her and she blushes. Because the security man she strategically flirted with sneaks her into Elvis's hotel suite. Because Elvis asks her who she is, because she says something about the press and UPI and Colonel Parker, and because he takes her by the hand, leads her into his bedroom, shuts the door, takes off his trousers, lies down on the bed and watches her as she undresses. They do it, up there on the twenty-fourth floor, and the whole time Gael can hear the girls on the street shouting 'We want Elvis'. The voices seem very far away.

Gael Greene writes about her date with Elvis long after she has become one of America's most prominent restaurant critics. Throughout the 1960s and 1970s, she explores the best establishments for *New York* magazine. She unites the sexual and culinary revolutions. According to Greene, the body parts involved in experiencing and registering pleasure at the table and in bed are the same. It is no coincidence that both of the following cross the lips: a lustful moan and an excellently roasted potato.

When it comes to the pleasure she experienced with Elvis, Gael Greene can't remember all the details. She does remember that soon after they finished the singer said he needed to sleep, that she got dressed in the bathroom – and that he then asked her to order a fried-egg sandwich for him from room service. What did Elvis look like naked? Was the sex good? Who was on top? She doesn't remember any of these details. The only thing that stuck in her memory was the fried-egg sandwich – she is a restaurant critic, after all.[18]

*

For the last quarter of a century, Alfred Kölling has been teaching trainees in the gastronomy trade. Now he is writing a book which aims to bring the waiters of the German Democratic Republic closer to the theory and practice of their profession. He joins forces with employees of the Mitropa railway-station restaurant in Leipzig. Kölling produces the text, while his Leipzig colleagues help with the illustrations. They demonstrate the correct and incorrect way to carry a napkin, how the first lengthways fold of the table linen should be executed, then how to make the second and third folds and bring the sides together. The polishing of a plate, the re-polishing of a knife, the re-polishing of forks: no detail is too small. Kölling advises the waiters on the appropriate way to care for their hair, teeth and feet, and details the tools of the trade: waiter's knife, cigar cutter, matchbox, sharpened pencils, notepad. He passes on his extensive knowledge of soups, egg dishes, fish, meat, tobacco products, beer and wine, and the correct setting of a breakfast table for a family with two children.

Kölling publishes his guidebook in 1956. It becomes a classic work. And it goes far beyond the details of cigar cutting. Kölling sees the waiter as a special figure in an egalitarian socialist society, in which the catering staff no longer represent the 'subservient spirit' of old, managed 'from the top down'. The waiter, according to Kölling, is now a colleague. Nonetheless, he still upholds the various codes which regulate the work: it is 'still the case that a good waiter should carry out his work in a friendly and attentive, tactful and honest, clean and conscientious manner'. An 'insight into human nature' is also indispensable. Nothing is more important than close observation of the customer: his gait and facial expression, his posture, his manner of expression and voice. There is the 'confident, decisive customer' and the 'unconfident, indecisive customer'. The spectrum of 'types' ranges from the friendly and talkative to the nervous, from the mistrustful to the pretentious. It's a complicated matter, warns Kölling in italics: '*The customers' moods are highly changeable*'. And so he returns to his basic theory, which defines the waiter as a model of attentiveness and emotional flexibility. He recommends the following: 'Diligent observation and changing gears as appropriate.'

There is just one instance where changing gears would never be appropriate. Kölling emphasizes that it is absolutely essential the waiter 'consistently represents the politics of the government of the German Democratic Republic'. He must agree with the government's political principles and their implementation, must recognize the 'gargantuan struggle' of the 'factory and farm workers' and admire the 'workers and members of the intelligentsia' just as much as the 'activists and working heroes'. And when he encounters a 'prominent' customer who plays a leading role in the state, a minister perhaps, familiar from the 'spotlight of public life' and 'demonstrations and large gatherings': the socialist waiter will 'discreetly' recommend a seat which will allow the well-known comrade to retreat from 'the gaze of curious diners'.[19]

*

Jacques Pépin has spent his military service working as a chef for President de Gaulle. Now he is leaving France. On 12 September 1959, he arrives in New York. He starts out in the best French restaurant in Manhattan: Le Pavillon. And he is less than impressed. American vegetables, fruit, herbs; nothing seems to be as flavoursome as in France. The beef isn't as firm. There is no lobster, no Mediterranean fish, no charcoal grill as he knows it from Parisian kitchens. Pépin is disappointed that, instead of the usual six cooks working as *entremetiers*, here there is only one – and all he really prepares is vegetable gratin. He is even more disappointed by the authoritarian gastronome Henri Soulé. Jacques sees him as a 'bombastic tyrant' whose shouting gets on his nerves.

But there is a much more fundamental problem. For years on end, the wages of the staff at Le Pavillon have not increased, supposedly due to the restaurant's financial situation. But when European aristocrats and film stars come in to dine, Soulé always gives them complimentary extras: caviar, champagne, desserts. And if someone's a really big name, they don't have to pay the bill at all.

Eight months after Pépin's arrival, conflict breaks out. The head chef is unable to tolerate Soulé any longer and hands in his notice. The other chefs want to follow him. So Jacques Pépin tries to import the French version of the worker's struggle to New York City: 'la brigade sauté'. All of the chefs, he declares, should simultaneously walk out of Le Pavillon.

The concept of 'la brigade sauté' reaches the ears of the powerful New York gastronomy workers' union. They respond by sending burly enforcers to the restaurant kitchen. The union representatives present scrawny Pépin with the choice of either abandoning the plan, or endangering his physical well-being and never being able to work in New York again. The argument is convincing and 'la brigade sauté' is dropped. But although the union enforcers can stop a mass walk-out, they can't prevent the chefs leaving one by one: which they do. Le Pavillon has to close down. And President de Gaulle's former chef must look for new employment.[20]

*

Restaurant owner Yoshiaki Shiraishi from Osaka has invented a mobile toilet. He is eternally curious, fond of tinkering. In 1953, he visits a brewery, where he stares, fascinated, at the conveyor belt transporting the beer bottles throughout the entire factory. Afterwards, he can't get that conveyor belt out of his mind. Five years after his brewery visit, he opens Genroku Sushi, a restaurant through which a steel band rotates in a clockwise direction. The conveyer belt carries the portions of sushi. Its speed is exactly eight centimetres per second. This is just the right tempo for the customers to look at the sushi, contemplate their choice and pick it up. A slower speed would be too frustrating, a quicker one too frantic. His plates of sushi circle like satellites, says Shiraishi in his promotional material, employing the language of the space age.

Sushi, originally only a snack food, and subsequently, in the pre-conveyor belt era, one of the most sophisticated dishes in Japan, becomes fast food again during the sixties and seventies – more democratic than aristocratic, and supported by the very latest technology. Genroku Sushi is efficient. The cooks don't have to wait for the customers, the customers don't have to wait for the food, and the subsequent customers

don't have to wait for the existing ones, who are instructed
to eat and clear their places as quickly as possible. Shiraishi's
business model spreads across Japan. His franchise system is
modelled on the successful strategies developed by American
burger chains.

The rise of sushi combines American technology with
Japanese tradition. It is driven by cultural and economic
globalization. Before the American occupation, the Japanese
regarded tuna as a second-rate fish. To them it was *abu* – too
fatty. But under the influence of the US soldiers and their
beloved steaks, Japanese taste buds change. Tuna fish is in
demand, especially for sushi: on Shiraishi's conveyor belts,
in bars and restaurants, first in Japan and then worldwide.[21]
It only takes a few decades before the fish is threatened with
extinction.[22]

*

Wolfram Siebeck, postwar German, discovers France. And he
finds it to be a great disappointment. He hitch-hikes to the
south, and all he can find are steaks with pommes frites. He
travels to Paris, can't afford any of its restaurants, eats tinned
sardines, drinks sweet, cheap wine. Heads back south again,
to the Côte d'Azur, where he is taken under the wing of a
gourmet who brings him to a supposedly excellent restaurant.
Maggots crawl in the chunks of cheese served as the final
course and the friendly gourmet gulps down cheese, maggots
and wine all at once. Young Wolfram Siebeck doesn't want
to touch it.

Books impress him more than these travels. In 1954, the
cookbook *What Men Like To Eat* is published. It leads Siebeck
away from the 'old German unimaginativeness'. Soon afterwards, he discovers Joseph Wechsberg, the elegant epicurean

writer, who opens up a 'previously unknown world' to him by comparing the 'content of pots and terrines with a Beethoven concert or one of Mozart's minuets'.[23] Siebeck soon switches from drawing to writing, begins to report on film festivals in France – and starts to have more luck. Now he finds restaurants which impress him. Which is he more enthusiastic about, avant-garde cinema or good food? That question isn't an easy one to answer.

*

On 1 February 1960, Joseph McNeil, David Richmond, Ezell Blair, Jr and Franklin McCain go out to eat together in Greensboro, North Carolina. They plan to meet at Woolworth's. In the restaurant section there, one can have lunch at an inviting counter, surrounded by pink tinted mirrors. All four of them are in their first year at the Agricultural and Technical College of North Carolina. But the aim of their excursion is not actually to have lunch. They are protesting against racial segregation in the American South, which dictates that they, as African Americans, cannot be served at a counter like the one in Woolworth's.

Franklin McCain simply wants to try something new. He is seventeen and later says: 'We wanted to go beyond what our parents had done.' Joseph McNeil is there because he knows the world outside of the South. His family lives in New York City. When he travels back to university after going home to see them, he notices that getting something to eat becomes more difficult with every city he passes. In Philadelphia, he can find a food stand anywhere at the bus station. In Richmond, Virginia, the hotdog stand is reserved for whites. And in Greensboro, further south, the racist codes are even stricter. The previous evening, the four of them were discussing the white domination of everyday life. And they spontaneously made the decision to do something about it.

And so they take their places at the 'white' counter. The African American waitress doesn't serve them and says: 'Fellows like you make our race look bad.' They stay sitting there, in front of the pink tinted mirrors, for the entire afternoon. In the South, any violation of the unwritten rules of segregation is a risk. Violence against black citizens is part of daily life. Five years before, a fourteen-year-old boy was lynched in Mississippi for speaking to a white woman.[24] But the four young men are gutsy.

*

Postwar German intellectuals attack the culture of consumerism and complacency. In 1960, Wolfgang Weyrauch writes: 'Prosperity has almost eaten us alive.' He accuses his contemporaries of eating 'instead of thinking', and declares that the role of the writer is to 'exercise criticism; passionate, self-exposing criticism'. *Zeitkritik* (the critical analysis of contemporary issues) becomes a catchword in a Federal Republic that can no longer avoid a serious, sophisticated critique of society's superficialities.[25] In West German intellectual history, the period of the early 1960s is regarded as the true beginning of the postwar years – its most prominent thinkers have a common aim: to transform society through the spirit of critical theory.[26]

Wolfram Siebeck, writer, intellectual, postwar German, produces cartoons for the magazine *twen*. First on the stands in 1959, it prioritizes creative layout and design, ambitious photojournalism and not-very-nuanced pornography. It reports from Provence, from Tuscany, and establishes these regions as the sought-after travel destinations for a new generation. A leftist writer compares *twen* to an 'advertising catalogue'.[27]

Siebeck's editor at *twen* is aware that his cartoonist has considerable cooking skills. And so, during the 1960s, he makes him a food columnist. Siebeck writes his first ever restaurant review (of Maxim's). He reports on a cookery course at the prestigious establishment Aux Armes de France in Alsatian Ammerschwihr. And, for the first time in his career as a journalist, he publishes a recipe. Prominently featured in the influential German magazine are his instructions for making *vitello tonnato*. Never before has this dish been described in the German language. Wolfram Siebeck, too, has made his contribution to German intellectual history.[28]

*

Nothing has happened to the four students at the Woolworth's counter. They haven't been served. Nor have they been attacked. That evening, they meet with other students to encourage them to join the protest. The next day, a Tuesday, twenty-three African American classmates sit at the 'whites only' counter. By Wednesday, there are eighty-five of them. The restaurant owners don't know what to do. Greensboro is a relatively liberal city, so they shy away from conflict. Only on Saturday, when four hundred students appear at Woolworth's, does the situation escalate. White youths and members of the Ku Klux Klan threaten the activists. Now the manager also threatens to call the police.

Lunch counters become the focal points of new forms of political protest. Previously, civil rights organizations were mostly reactive: to racist crimes, to cases of discrimination. Established lawyers or preachers like Martin Luther King, Jr led civil rights protests. But the students sitting at the counter in Woolworth's are young, and they don't want to keep waiting for something to happen. They are acting instead of reacting. They aren't hiding behind leading personalities. And they do more than just make the staff on the other side of the counter nervous; they inspire activism across the entire South.[29]

In Nashville, Tennessee, James Lawson starts to train young people for restaurant sit-ins. They learn how they should go up to and away from the counter, how to keep chairs free when someone has to go to the bathroom, and also how they should dress: the male participants in a suit and tie, the women in stockings and high-heeled shoes. Only a few days after the impromptu action in Greensboro, sit-ins take place in Nashville. All across the city, young African Americans sit at restaurant counters reserved for whites and ask to be served.

The movement spreads through thirty-one additional cities: it is conceived to be a long-term and consistent action. It also becomes a model for white student protests. And in Greensboro, the epicentre, the sit-in is successful. A short while later, the Woolworth's restaurant is opened to both black and white customers.

In September 1960, six months after the first protest, Joseph McNeil, one of the four pioneers of the protest movement, returns to Greensboro. He is beginning his second year of studies. The goal has been accomplished. So he goes to eat at the now historic lunch counter at Woolworth's and sits down once more in front of the pink-tinted mirrors. But the choice of dishes is uninspiring, McNeill finds, and even the apple pie he has for dessert isn't particularly good.[30]

*

Beluga caviar and vodka: this is the first course Joseph Wechsberg is served. In 1962, he is sitting at a long table of the now reopened Le Pavillon in Manhattan. Next comes Mousse de Saumon-Poulette, then Filet de Boeuf Financière (with a 1947 Château Cheval Blanc), Poularde Froide à la Neva and Salade Gauloise as the fourth course, then Fromages de France served with a Magnum of Dom Perignon. To round things off, Wechsberg can look forward to a Sorbet Héricart and Friandises, as well as an exceptional Marc de Bourgogne. And the most exceptional and enjoyable part is that he doesn't have to pay the bill. The celebratory meal for him and his nineteen guests is on the house.[31]

Wechsberg has more than earned it. He wrote a long article about Le Pavillon for the *New Yorker* which grew into an entire book, exploring every facet of the establishment. Or more precisely: every positive facet. Wechsberg almost completely ignores the complex labour conflicts at Le Pavillon. Instead, he composes an ode to the most exquisite restaurant he can imagine. He praises the new head chef Clement Grangier as a 'gentleman' of the kitchen, who simmers his mother sauces for no less than forty-eight hours. He lovingly portrays Grangier's copper pans. He praises the accommodating treatment of prominent guests – for instance, how John F. Kennedy is served his favourite drink, cold milk, in a silver champagne bucket.

First and foremost, however, Wechsberg dishes out compliments to Henri Soulé, the owner of Pavillon. Jacques Pépin depicted Soulé as a bellowing tyrant. Wechsberg, gourmet and music-lover, instead compares him to a great conductor, distributing his guests amongst the restaurant's tables as if they are part of a complex musical interpretation. In this way, everyone's status is maintained and the atmosphere is as glamorous as possible. Wechsberg is impressed by the highly diplomatic finesse with which Soulé handles impertinent customers, and his detached manner towards excessively pandering gourmets. And the writer takes particular pleasure in the fact that he himself has not only been a guest at Soulé's summer home on occasion, but has also enjoyed a few hotdogs on the street with the maestro.

Joseph Wechsberg is a regular commuter between Europe and the United States, and he always visits Le Pavillon before he sets off to the Old World. The vast majority of his articles explore the world of beauty, elegance and luxury, and portray the connoisseurs of excellent hotels, expensive violins and refined dishes.[32]

Wechsberg is an excellent fit for the publication which has given him a professional home in the USA. The *New Yorker* of the American postwar era defines itself as a guardian of civilization. It points the way towards the most cultivated products and ideas, enabling its readers to set themselves apart from the tastelessness of mass culture, and sees itself as the voice of idealized American democracy. Paranoid anti-communists they are not, but they are very much convinced of the United States' uniqueness.[33]

To Wechsberg, Pavillon is not only a restaurant, but also a symbol of the splendour of American consumer society. He treasures the thick carpets and white tablecloths, the Baccarat glasses and depictions of the Champs-Élysées which decorate the walls. He savours the Consommé Royale, cooked for four whole hours, and the Bombe Pavillon, a dessert made from vanilla and coffee ice cream, pears, apples, peaches and pineapple, all drenched in cherry liqueur and flambéed. The scent of Beurre Noisette and expensive perfume brings him to the ironic conclusion that, at Le Pavillon, one can experience the 'triumph of evil capitalism and good taste'.

And yet the Bombe Pavillon hasn't totally mollified the critical intellectual in Joseph Wechsberg. On occasion, he concedes, the restaurant's prices attest to the injustice of Western civilization. After all, he writes, for the cost of one dinner in this establishment, a 'great deal of food could be bought for the starving children in Africa or the hungry farmers of China'. It is a moral issue, one which Wechsberg almost faces up to and then swiftly evades, in true Cold War spirit. Anyone who raises these arguments, he claims, would be overlooking the fact that there are equally exclusive banquets in the Eastern bloc, except that there only the communist leaders have access to the top restaurants. Wechsberg sees Le Pavillon, by contrast, as an open, democratic establishment. No one who wants to spend their money there would ever be turned away.[34]

*

It is 28 May 1963. Later on this day, two youths will tear Anne Moody from her seat at the counter of a department-store restaurant, grab her hair and drag her the ten metres to the exit. A few hours after this, she will enter a beauty salon and ask the hairdresser there to wash the ketchup, mustard and sugar out of her hair. And that evening she will walk through the doors of Pearl Street Church in Jackson, Mississippi, where the benches are filled to the very last seat, and everyone will applaud her for minutes on end.

For now, she doesn't yet know any of this. At exactly eleven o'clock in the morning, she walks into the Woolworth's store in Jackson with her two classmates, Memphis and Pearlena. They separate at the entrance, look around briefly, then buy a few things. At 11.14 they meet near the restaurant section. Shortly before 11.15, the three women take their seats at the counter, as planned.

In Greensboro, the college students' sit-ins began spontaneously and quickly led to success. But the culture of racial segregation in the American South cannot be overcome in just a few weeks. There are immense differences between

North Carolina, a comparatively liberal state, and a town like Jackson, far down in the South, in Mississippi. No one knows what will happen today. So the activists are well prepared. Anne Moody is the group's spokeswoman. The police and press have been informed.

Anne and her two fellow students try to order. The waitress points them towards the 'black' part of the counter. Anne replies that they want to be served here, in the 'white' part. The waitress immediately turns off the light at the counter and flees, probably afraid that violence will break out.

She is wrong – or at least so it seems. A white girl at the counter next to Anne sees no reason to leave and instead calmly eats her banana split. Another white woman goes up to the activists and says that she would like to stay with them, but unfortunately her husband is expecting her. Reporters enter the restaurant area. They take photographs. They ask questions. Anne says: 'All we want is service.' Everything is calm.

The situation changes when white high-school students come into Woolworth's during the lunch hour. They swear loudly at the three young women at the counter. They find a rope, knot it into a noose and try to lasso their heads. More and more whites, students and grown-ups, stream into the store and threaten the activists. Anne, Memphis and Pearlena pray in an attempt to stay calm, but that really riles up the crowd. The black students are thrown to the ground, punched and kicked. Memphis is taken away by a policeman. Anne and Pearlena sit back up at their seats. The mob calls them communists. Anne is dragged away. She comes back to the counter again. The crowd smear her with mustard and ketchup, throw cakes and sugar at her. Dozens of policemen stand in front of Woolworth's and do nothing. Only when the president of Anne's college appears and negotiates their safe retreat do they leave their places at the counter. In front of the shop, onlookers pelt them once more, with all kinds of objects.

In her autobiography, Anne Moody later writes that she had always hated the whites in Mississippi, but that after that morning at the Woolworth's counter, the hate ceased. That was the day she realized these people were suffering from an 'illness': an 'incurable illness' in its final throes.[35]

*

Rolf Anschütz is looking for chairs. He spends the winter of 1965/6 climbing into the attics of old inns. Anschütz, a resident of Suhl, Thuringia, in the German Democratic Republic, has recently had a career setback. He has been demoted from his role as 'district director of gastronomy' to being merely a restaurant manager. It seems that someone up there in the communist hierarchy doesn't like him. Despite successfully completing his long-distance learning course to become a gastronomic engineer-economist two years previously, he's now in charge of a run-of-the-mill place called Waffenschmied in Suhl's Gothaer Strasse. At least he finds the chairs he is looking for, and he saws the legs off suitable specimens. He does the same with a small round table, before nailing it on to two bottle crates and covering it with waxed paper.[36]

In the mid-1960s, socialist East Germany gives its citizens more leisure time by reducing working hours. Every second weekend, there is now a work-free Saturday. Due to the cramped housing conditions, people are driven outside on these days: into cafés and restaurants. Rolf Anschütz, though frustrated by his demotion, wants to offer something to his fellow citizens. He may be just an employee of a trade organization, running a restaurant that isn't even his own, but it is his purpose in life nonetheless.[37] He saws off the chair legs and upcycles the tables because he wants to set up a Japanese space in the restaurant: a menu of Far-Eastern specialities within Waffenschmied, previously known for its simple and hearty German comfort food. He doesn't have a Japanese cookbook, but he has gathered the necessary knowledge at the hotel school in Leipzig, in the 'World Cuisines' module. He knows one dish: Sukiyaki. The ingredients are available in Suhl: beef, wild mushrooms, onions, white cabbage. And so he begins the tradition of the Suhl Japanese evenings. His guests eat – and sit – as though they are in the Land of the Rising Sun.

When, through some twist of fate, an actual Japanese diner eats at Waffenschmied, he shares a recipe with Anschütz and has produce sent to him from East Asia. Now Anschütz is able to cook a second dish. In 1966, the first Japanese journalists come to visit his restaurant. This heralds the beginning of a long intercultural relationship. Anschütz begins to research the Shinto faith. He learns that Japan was isolated from the rest of the world for two whole centuries, a country as sealed off as the German Democratic Republic, and that soon after its opening to the West in the late nineteenth century, it gravitated towards German culture. This is the story which the Suhl banquets are intended to represent. 'I may live in Germany,' Rolf Anschütz will later say, 'but my soul lives in Japan.'[38]

*

In 1970, Jacques Pépin, former apprentice in Bourg-en-Bresse, completes his BA at Columbia University. His final thesis explores the work of Molière. He pursues his academic career further: a Masters in eighteenth-century French literature is his next goal, after which he wants to do a PhD.

Pépin has turned down an offer to cook for the Kennedys at the White House. He is now working for one of the biggest restaurant chains of the day: Howard Johnson's. In a gigantic warehouse complex in Queens, he develops new recipes for the company's numerous branches. He is involved with something most top French chefs find unthinkable: his meals are deep frozen, then defrosted and reheated in the restaurants before serving. Pépin's team uses saucepans which hold almost 4,000 litres. They can produce 2,500 portions of Boeuf Bourguignon in one go. In a single day, they debone 1,500 turkeys. Their recipe for veal stock calls for 3,000 American pounds of veal bones, 200 pounds of onions, 100 pounds of celery, 150 pounds of carrots, 44 litres of tinned tomatoes, two bags of salt and a pound of peppercorns. Pépin sees himself as a 'soldier' in the American 'food revolution'. He claims that this position has opened up a 'whole new world of culinary possibilities' to him. The Americans, he says, and especially the Howard Johnson customers, are so much more open-minded than the French.[39]

The academic world, however, is not so tolerant. As a student who now has all the necessary prerequisites for a PhD, Jacques Pépin suggests a topic to his supervisor. He wants to combine the study of literature and his experiences in the kitchen: he has drafted out a study of food in French literature. He wants to progress from Pierre de Ronsard's sixteenth-century 'Ode to a Salad', via the wedding breakfast in Flaubert's *Madame Bovary* to Proust's reflections on the madeleine. His literature professor rejects the proposal. Too trivial, he explains.[40]

*

In Berkeley, California, Alice Waters is assembling the workforce for her restaurant. A graduate student in Italian studies is acting as co-manager. A PhD student of philosophy, who has never worked in a restaurant before, becomes the head chef. A composer and music critic takes on the role of bartender. As *pâtissièr*, Waters has hired a friend who, like her, has a degree in French cultural history.

At the opening on 28 August 1971, Waters' Chez Panisse offers only a set menu, following the model of simple French restaurants: Pâte en croûte, Canard aux olives. Plum tart is served for dessert. The price is $3.95. Two weeks later, the staff will be informed in writing that unfortunately their wages cannot yet be paid in full, that each of them will receive 10 per cent of the agreed sum – and that those who don't urgently need this 10 per cent should kindly return it so that it can be distributed to those of their co-workers who are in financial need.[41]

Chez Panisse will go on to become the most influential restaurant in the United States, and Alice Waters will become an international star of the slow-food movement. More than thirty years after its opening, the journalist George Packer will cite the restaurant as a symbol of a self-obsessed American elite to whom culinary finesse and organic purity are more important than the country's swiftly intensifying social inequality. He calls Waters the 'radish queen'.[42] At the same time, a team of economists will study Chez Panisse and declare it to be a shining example of an 'open innovation-ecosystem', an economic model built upon shared knowledge, trust between its employees and continued personal development amongst the workforce.[43]

For now, these interpretations remain in the distant future. Financial difficulties will continue to grip Chez Panisse for decades – not least because Alice Waters seems to lack good business sense. She doesn't want to add additional tables to make more money; the dining room should continue to be furnished in as minimalist a way as possible. Customers are constantly being treated to items on the house, sometimes champagne, sometimes dessert, sometimes their entire meal. In the first year of the restaurant's existence, the staff knock back $30,000 worth of wine. Drug-taking is part of the normal working day. But one factor is fundamental both to Chez Panisse's financial difficulties as well as its cultural significance: Alice Waters is uncompromising when it comes to the quality of the food. The ingredients always have to be the best.

Chez Panisse symbolizes a much larger movement: away from industrialized gastronomy and back to supposed simplicity. Regional cooking comes back to life. Foraging is back: herbs from friends' gardens, cress from rivers and streams, fennel from the side of the road. Alice Waters brings a French concept to California: that of *terroir* and its unique significance to life and to pleasure. The student revolts are a thing of the past. Now, young academics, co-workers at Chez Panisse, are searching for blackberries along the Berkeley railway embankment.[44]

*

A simple salad of green beans and tomatoes at Paul Bocuse, frogs' legs with herbs at the Troisgros Brothers: these are the dishes referenced by Henri Gault and Christian Millau as they construct their very own French revolution. Forgotten flavour notes, simplicity and lightness have, according to Gault/Millau, created a 'new cuisine'. This concept has arisen again and again throughout gastronomical history. Even Voltaire once complained that his stomach couldn't handle the 'nouvelle cuisine'. But it is particularly appropriate at a time when French literature is dominated by the *nouveau roman* and cinema by the *nouvelle vague*.[45]

In 1973, Gault and Millau create the 'Ten Commandments of Nouvelle Cuisine'. Some rules are very concrete. They stress the importance of not overcooking, of using fresh, high-quality ingredients, serving light fare, not using any marinades, no hung game, no fermentation, no brown or white sauces. Then again, the authors become philosophical too. One must be 'systématique moderniste', they declare. Tricks in the presentation are to be avoided, but the tenth and most important rule says: 'Tu seras inventif.'[46]

French cuisine changes as a result. Menus become simpler, flavour is intensified, freshness dominates. No longer is carving or flambéeing carried out at the table. The plate gains importance. Each guest receives his own, individual, freshly prepared work of art, with echoes of ornamental Japanese art or the paintings of Mirò and Kandinsky.

The neatly arranged portions are part of a comprehensive change of image. Everything associated with the restaurant is to be defined no longer by excess, but instead by leanness and efficiency. The chef Michel Guérard, for example, represents *cuisine minceur*, calorie-reduced cooking.[47] To body-conscious Americans, this version of nouvelle cuisine becomes its representative form.[48] Gael Greene visits Guérard's restaurant and eats chicken on cucumber purée with spinach and pear foam. She loses, she claims, nine American pounds in ten days.[49]

Gault and Millau's gift for invention is also commercially profitable. Restaurant critics and chefs work closely together. The more sensational the new cuisine depicted in its pages, the greater the sales figures for the *Gault & Millau* culinary almanac (first published in 1969). And the more readers the almanac wins, the more tiny-portion-seeking diners appear in restaurants. The respective histories of the media and gastronomy industries unite particularly well in the pages of modern glossy magazines, where a new generation of food photographers are coming to the fore. Plates become backgrounds for geometric arrangements, and these arrangements become logos for enterprising cooks.[50] Paul Bocuse, not a pioneer of the new style of cooking, though consistently associated with it, attributes the growing status of his profession to the sea change initiated by Gault and Millau. 'Once we were servants, now we are owners,' he explains. The occasion: at Elysée Palace, Bocuse has just been made a member of the National Legion d'Honneur.[51]

*

Huge grill platters: that's what the restaurant Talbot is famous for. In Worcestershire, at least. Most of the other main dishes come from plastic sachets. Boeuf bourguignon, coq au vin, duck à l'orange, cordon bleu: they all wait their turn in the deep freezer until a customer orders them.

Nigel's job, at which today is his first day, consists of fetching the plastic bags from the freezer. Further tasks are soon added. Due to the fact that the sachets' stick-on labels have gone astray, he has to differentiate between the deep-frozen coq and the deep-frozen duck by means of detailed groping. He defrosts prawns in hot water. He decorates pies with parsley and orange zest, fixes lemon slices to the rim of crab cocktail glasses, decorates fruit cakes with rosettes of cream.

Nigel is fifteen years old and it is his first time working in a restaurant kitchen. He will come back the next day. Soon, he starts to love his work so much that he finds his days off depressing. It gets him from away his family: his father and his father's new partner, whom Nigel finds unbearable. In the restaurant kitchen, he finds a new family: a lively tribe, who meet each Sunday to have a staff meal and make fun of the customers.

This gastronomic family allows him to grow. From Diane the cook he learns how to roast potatoes so they get really crispy on the outside and fluffy on the inside, how to grill rump steak, fillet steak, how to make onion rings, how to prepare Irish coffee, how to put together crab cocktail sauce (mayonnaise, ketchup, a little chopped parsley and just a touch of paprika – such an exotic spice isn't particularly popular with the Talbot clientele). He learns that although iceberg lettuce doesn't taste of much, it keeps for a long time and is therefore preferred in this kitchen above all other salad leaves. And he learns, although not from his superiors, that one can buy oneself sex by secretly siphoning off steak and drinks for a girl called Julia and serving them to her in the parking lot behind the restaurant.

Then his father dies, collapsing during a tennis game. And so this time comes to an end, because now he has to move on, away from this world. But the pubescent Nigel, that kitchen novice in Worcestershire, will a few decades later become England's best-loved food writer. Nigel Slater makes the Talbot a key location in his food-filled autobiography *Toast*, with chapters entitled 'Scrambled Egg', 'Lemon Sherbets', 'Ham' and 'Cheese and Onion Crisps'. The *Independent* calls Slater 'the Proust of the Nesquik era'.[52]

*

Numerous explosions go off in St Louis, Missouri. It is 16 March 1972, a few minutes after three in the afternoon. An entire housing development is destroyed. Nobody is hurt. At least not today. In the past, innumerable people have suffered in this development, called Pruitt-Igoe. At the time of its inauguration in 1955, it was lauded as a housing project of the future, yet it became one of the worst slums in the

United States: a hotspot of drug dealers, poverty and crime. The demolition of Pruitt-Igoe is seen by some as the end of architectonic modernity.[53]

Pruitt-Igoe was designed by the American architect Minoru Yamasaki. Now he has once again been entrusted with an extremely important commission. He is to give New York City a facelift, one that will be seen all over America, and indeed the whole world. In one section of the building, Yamasaki plans a two-storey restaurant, on the 106th and 107th floors, with a breathtaking view. Here, glass and steel will once more have the spectacular impact dreamed of by the pioneers of modernism.

Critical urbanists see things differently: to them, the project destroys the human scale of the dense, vibrant metropolis. They see an unparalleled collaboration between the economic oligarchy and corrupt politicians, in the service of global capitalism.[54]

Construction goes ahead regardless. Yamasaki erects the complex exactly where, in the late nineteenth and early twentieth centuries, the so-called Syrian quarter was located, a neighbourhood filled with shops and restaurants owned by Arabic immigrants. The area once looked like a bazaar. *Flâneurs* admired oriental textiles and jars. Restaurants offered kebabs, baklava and knafeh.[55] Those days are now long gone.

The New York Port Authority, responsible for the construction of the new complex, imagines the gastronomic zone high up in the skyscraper as a private club: accessible only to their own management people and their associates in the Downtown Lower Manhattan Association. Loud protests ensue. It is a little hard to explain why New York taxpayers are subsidizing this monumental construction but are not allowed to go and eat there. In the end, planners decide that the 106th and 107th floors will be open to the public after all.[56]

There are two thousand suggestions for what to name the restaurant. Someone hears Catarina Valente sing 'The Windows of the World' and concludes that this, with a slight tweak, will do just fine.[57] Windows on the World, inaugurated on 19 April 1976, turns into one of the most commercially successful restaurants in the United States. It takes in $37 million in the year 2000 and is destroyed on 11 September 2001, high above the neighbourhood once known for its Arabic restaurants.[58]

*

Truman Capote is working on a novel which is intended in the same mode as Marcel Proust's *In Search of Lost Time*. He wants to compose a portrait of late twentieth-century society and thought. One of the scenes takes place on 55th Street in Manhattan, at Côte Basque, an offshoot of Le Pavillon. Two people are sitting at a table: Ina Coolbirth, society lady, and the narrator, a man named Jonesy. Capote devotes forty pages to describing their lunch.

The gastronome Soulé appears – praised by Joseph Wechsberg, despised by Jacques Pépin. Capote depicts him as a sweating snob, 'pink and shiny like a marzipan pig'. Soulé recommends the lamb to the two diners. They ignore his suggestion and order the Soufflé Furstenberg: a mixture of cheese, spinach and eggs. They drink two bottles of champagne, Roederer Cristal. It isn't cold enough, but it does the job.

The quality of the food is irrelevant, excepting one brief moment when Capote has Lady Ina inspect a salad leaf through her dark sunglasses. What matters is the location of their table. They are seated not in the rear of the room, but, as is typical in sophisticated restaurants of that time, towards the front, close to the entrance, where everything happens, where one sees everyone, where one sits if one is a somebody. Their conversation is important, much more important than the soufflé. They exchange the worst sort of society gossip. About Cole Porter's hand wrapped around an Italian sommelier's penis, about the woman who wanted to marry Orson Welles when she was sixteen years old and then exchanged love letters with J. D. Salinger. About Joe Kennedy, Jackie's ex-father-in-law, who raped Lady Ina at the Kennedy's family residence and liked the fact that she didn't scream. About Jackie Kennedy, who Lady Ina claims is nothing but a Western geisha and who Jonesy believes is a drag queen playing Jackie Kennedy. About an elite society lady who, out of sheer anti-Semitic antipathy, soiled the bed of a Jewish would-be-lover with her menstrual blood. About the very same gentleman in Lake Garda, his bathing shorts around his knees, a penis (his own) in his hand. About Anne Hopkins, who shot her unfaithful husband in the shower and got away with it. At this very moment, she is sitting a few tables away, deep in conversation with a priest.

More and more stories, more and more vulgarities flow into Capote's tale. Then the champagne kicks in. Lady Ina gets the hiccups, Henri Soulé sends them a reprimanding glare, and all of a sudden lunch is over. Lady Ina stands up. And she looks, writes Capote, like a dolphin leaping out of the ocean. She pushes back the table, knocks over a champagne glass and stumbles towards the ladies' toilets. The waiters of Côte Basque reset the table for the evening service. For the reader, it is an 'atmosphere of luxurious exhaustion'.[59]

*

The male and female restaurant customers use separate changing rooms. Once undressed, the women adjourn to the bathing pool first, followed by the men. The guests sit in the water with one another – and for Rolf Anschütz, the East German restaurant manager, this is a very special moment of equality: 'Wealth, social status, professional standing – all these things are irrelevant here in the pool.' Given that 'only people's heads could be seen peeking out of the water,' the gastronome later adds, 'no one knew who was who.'

Anschütz expanded the Waffenschmied in Suhl to include a bathing pool in 1975. This is in keeping with the tradition of inns in Japan, where diners bathe before the meal, allowing the water to wash away the dirt from the street outside and dissolve the worries of daily life. Here in Thuringia, unlike in East Asia, the female guests giggle and wolf-whistle as the men approach the pool. By this point, Rolf Anschütz has already been serving Japanese specialities for more than a decade. Because his restaurant brings in foreign currency and invigorates the relationship between the GDR and Japan, the authorities give him special treatment. A restaurateur in a socialist country where even the simplest goods are often unattainable, he receives exotic products for Waffenschmied from Düsseldorf, and, from 1977 onwards, directly from Japan itself. The GDR and Japan establish diplomatic relations in 1973, and Waffenschmied serves as a figurehead, a representative of openness and internationality.

After the bathing ceremony, first the men, then the women withdraw from the pool, pull their undergarments back on, clothe themselves in polyester kimonos and stride towards the Japanese banquet. The men appear first, then the women. The East Asian ceremonies are explained to them. Irene Albrecht, a key figure of the local party leadership, refuses the kimono and eats in her street clothes. She regards the Japanese banquet with its cleansing bath as 'poppycock' the working classes have no need for.[60]

*

In the autumn of 1975, *Esquire* magazine will publish 'La Côte Basque 1965', the first instalment of Truman Capote's planned novel. By 10 October, Ann Woodward has already discovered that she will be identified in the extract as a murderess. After reading an advance copy, she commits suicide.

When the magazine appears on the stands, readers quickly see the connections between Capote's supposedly fictional protagonists and actual members of New York's high society. Slim Keith, a good friend of Capote's, recognizes herself in the drinking, gossiping Ina Coolbirth. The targets of her gossip are just as easily decoded. The cover of *New York* magazine swiftly features a caricature of an aggressive little dog in the middle of elegant human society. 'Capote bites the hands that fed him' proclaims the caption. The erstwhile darling of the rich and famous loses his society contacts. All his attempts to win them back fail.

This autumn is a turning point in Capote's biography: the beginning of a long personal crisis. And yet the author stands by his literary treatment of Soufflé Furstenberg and champagne, and the gossip. As an artist, he is defined only by his art, he says. As a writer, he had to write what he knew. 'Oh, honey!' he says to the fashion journalist Diana Vreeland, trying to explain his literary strategy to her: 'It's Proust! It's beautiful!'[61]

*

In the autumn of 1975, Craig Claiborne first has some luck and then an excellent idea. He wins a dinner voucher for two from a television tombola. The sponsor is American Express. There is no price limit. To be used in any restaurant of his choice. Claiborne thinks this would make a nice story for the *New York Times*. He isn't a Fluffo PR man any more, nor has he been for a long while: instead, he is now the food editor of the most revered newspaper in America. He is a critic and lifestyle expert, an authority on all things culinary. Now, with the help of the voucher, he starts to plan the most expensive restaurant visit of all time.

Having the dinner in New York would be too close to home. So he sets off to Paris with his good friend in tow, the chef Pierre Franey. At Chez Denis, an exclusive insider's tip, they find just the place they are looking for. And they really go to town.

Thirty-one courses and nine wines are presented to Claiborne and Franey. They start with Beluga caviar, followed by three different soups, oysters, lobster, a Provençal red mullet cake, Bresse pigeon, sorbets. Ortolans: little birds fed exclusively on berries for the duration of their short lives. Exquisite to eat, bones, head and all, everything except the legs. Almost an entire ortolan, a buttery mouthful, disappears between Craig Claiborne's lips. Then some wild duck glides in after it, followed by veal sirloin in puff pastry, served with golfball-sized black truffles. Artichoke purée. Duck liver in aspic. Woodcock breast. Cold pheasant with fresh hazelnuts. And then the deserts: a Raspberry Charlotte, Pear Alma, an Île Flottante, accompanied by a 1928 Château d'Yquem. This, in turn, makes way for an 1835 Madeira which accompanies the dessert courses. Followed by a 100-year-old Calvados with the coffee.

The men are not entirely satisfied. Claiborne found the lobster a little tough, and the sauce that accompanied the oysters was more lukewarm than hot. The pheasant wasn't that convincing either. And the presentation of the sweetbread parfait and the quail mousse tart? Rather slapdash.

Nonetheless: remaining ecstatic for the duration of thirty-one courses is an impossible feat. Allowing for this, Claiborne and Franey draw a positive conclusion overall. And Claiborne sets to work on describing the dinner in detail and with great gusto for the *New York Times*.

His article is published on 14 November 1975. The title reveals the price of the most exquisite dinner in human history: $4,000 – at that time, the cost of a good, factory-new middle-class car. The *Times* readers are not impressed; Claiborne's article comes out during the depths of the 1970s economic crisis. Inflation has the United States in its grip and New York in particular is badly affected. The city is fighting high unemployment, a massive crime problem and a budgetary situation which makes bankruptcy seem inevitable. This is a historic caesura for the entire United States: the era of postwar prosperity is coming to an end. The wages of workers and middle-class employees are stagnating. De-industrialization begins, companies begin to outsource jobs to countries with lower wages. Social inequality increases rapidly.[62]

More than 250 letters arrive in the editorial office within the first five days after the article's publication. Most of the letter writers consider Claiborne's dinner to be abhorrent – decadent, vulgar, frivolous, especially considering the millions of starving people in the world. Some show understanding, coming to Claiborne's defence. But for every positive letter there are four more expressing disgust. In total, over 1,000 readers' letters will be received.

Claiborne later reports that even the Vatican denounced the dinner in Chez Denis as 'scandalous'. He, however, stands by his project, pointing out that he didn't take food away from someone who was starving. And he clears up a further question – no, he didn't give a tip; as far as he was concerned it was already included.[63]

*

Anthropologists Michael Nicod and Gerald Mars are joining forces in order to research English waiters. The project, they say, is as complex as researching a mountain tribe in New Guinea. Nicod becomes a waiter himself for the purpose of the assignment, and discusses his observations with Mars. They cite William Foote Whyte as one of their role models, who in their opinion always succeeded in achieving just the right balance between distance and over-identification.[64] They approach the topic in a highly reflective way, taking great pains to remain consistently objective.

But this is a difficult undertaking. Michael Nicod, not quite the detached scholar, notes how deeply disappointed he feels when he is passed over for promotion from busboy to regular waiter.[65] Like George Orwell half a century before him, he too has to make some cosmetic concessions: on one occasion he gets a job only on the condition that he shaves off his moustache and cuts his hair. This is one of the findings of Mars and Nicod's study: the higher the status of a British hotel restaurant, the less hair its male waiters are permitted.[66]

It is the waiters' pinching of foodstuffs which strikes Nicod the most. They are constantly taking cheese, marmalade, tea and sugar home with them from the workplace. One buys fillet steaks cheaply from a chef and sells them in a neighbouring restaurant. Others hide smoked salmon in their trousers when they go home for the day. In one hotel, a waiter smuggles a cake out of the restaurant and sells it slice by slice to the guests in the lounge. Customers are served cheap drinks and given expensive bills. The larger the group, the easier the trickery. A group orders twelve bottles of wine – only eleven are put on the table. If one gin and tonic contains only half the dosage of juniper spirit, no one will notice – as long as a little is rubbed around the rim of the glass. This is the last phase before the computerization of gastronomy. For now, the waiters can still exercise creativity with the bills in their quest to lighten people's pockets.

Mars and Nicod explore territories also described by Erving Goffman. Any newcomer to the group of cheating waiters will eventually reach a point when the cheating no longer seems to him as such, but instead simply an activity which is part of him and his world.[67] The waiters cheat because they earn so little money – and because the other waiters are cheating too, because it becomes a normal part of their activities, because it feels right. Only Michael Nicod doesn't take part in the great cheating game. In one establishment, he almost blows his cover by reading a sociology book during his break. The title: *The Professional Thief.*[68]

*

Wolfram Siebeck arrives in Würzburg by train and goes to eat in the station restaurant. He is a very busy man. He eats and writes, eats and writes, for a gourmet magazine, for Germany's most important weekly. He eats and writes so much that the German poet Günter Herburger has written a poem which begins with the lines: *Let us simply forbid Wolfram Siebeck/ from writing about food.* Instead, Herburger fantasizes, Siebeck should be left in the Würzburg railway-station restaurant for three days 'with his mouth taped shut'. In order to respond to this demand, Siebeck has come to Würzburg. He sits and orders.

Other appointments in his diary are more spectacular – but not necessarily any more satisfying. He attends an event celebrating gourmet French cuisine in Château Vizille, the finale of which features a raft, coming down the river, carrying a 4-metre-high chocolate pyramid complete with decorative young women. The raft almost capsizes. He eats once more at Maxim's and is so disappointed by the dishes that he claims the high point of the evening to be the 'exquisite perfumes in the restaurant bathroom'. In Paul Bocuse's restaurant he sees 'pastry towers, sauce puddles, calorie bombs', and compares the kitchen with that of a truck stop. In response, Bocuse directs some choice words at him during their next encounter. Less surprising is Siebeck's disappointment in the restaurant car of the German national railway, where he finds the Beaujolais too warm, the herring too cold, the consistency of the pot roast reminiscent of a 'soggy box of cigars' and that of the rump steak akin to a 'tough old shoe sole'. In 1985 he receives the Golden Goblet of the German Hotel and Inn Association and uses his acceptance speech as an opportunity to launch an attack on flour-based sauces. He also attacks those of his contemporaries who regard themselves as critical gourmets 'simply because they once spat up some spinach on their mothers' aprons'.

In the Würzburg railway-station restaurant, Siebeck eats veal ragout with 'tough and ropy' meat. He tries the goulash soup, 'brown and mushy in a steel cup', and a filet steak, the 'mealy consistency' of which betrays its origins: the deep freezer. Here and there he goes off on a tangent, meditating on the oversized young Würzberg peas, and on the 'plump behinds and nurse-like bosoms' of the 'young girls' of the mid-seventies. Then he leaves before dessert.[69]

*

Twenty years have passed since Gael Green's rendezvous with Elvis. Now, in May 1976, she is in Windows on the World, high up in the World Trade Center, in order to review the restaurant in the new towers for *New York* magazine. She stares in wonder and amazement. At the 'heroic blue sweep' of the harbour below, at the bridge, at New Jersey. Yes, even New Jersey looks good from up here. She feels intoxicated, spellbound, no longer cynical, no longer paranoid. She is going to write that this place, Windows on the World, turned her into a different person. It is, she says, 'the most spectacular restaurant in the world', a 'dizzying post-industrial enchantment'. Hate and fear, she declares, are invisible here.[70]

One of Gael Greene's colleagues, Mimi Sheraton, is also dining in the North Tower of the World Trade Center. She is representing the *New York Times*. She finds the quail egg aspic too stiff ('like a paperweight') and the eggplant too salty. The zucchini are burnt. The lamb, which should have been pink, is almost raw, the raspberries partly unripe and partly rotten.[71]

Gael Greene considers the food in Windows on the World to be irrelevant. The restaurant is a triumph regardless, she writes. 'Money and power and ego and a passion for perfection' made this place possible. And money, power and ego could also help the entire city of New York out of the crisis. Greene eats, drinks, interviews the restaurant manager Joe Baum, admires the waiters' uniforms and speaks with Jacques Pépin, who is consultant chef for the Windows on the World kitchen. The elevator which brings her back to the ground floor, back to reality, takes fifty-eight seconds. But even here she's delighted: this elevator, she says, is the same height as one and a half Clint Eastwoods.[72]

*

Now Mimi Sheraton is eating in Paul Bocuse's restaurant near Lyon. She is not particularly impressed. The duck breast is tough and salty. The gâteau de foies de volailles tastes more

like calves' liver, and she finds the interior decor of the restaurant vulgar. She also stops off at the lauded L'Oustau de
Baumanière in Les Baux and finds the dry lamb there just
as disappointing as the lobster bisque. At the legendary La
Pyramide in Vienne, she finds the food even sadder. The owner,
she feels, wanders through the restaurant like a soulless robot.

Mimi Sheraton is Craig Claiborne's successor at the *New
York Times*. He doesn't like her. She doesn't like him. He is a
gentleman, a friend of the top chefs, a Southern aesthete, who
during his childhood was cooked for by African American
servants and talks about it as though he grew up during the
slavery era.[73] Sheraton, a middle-class Brooklynite, sees herself
as a representative of ordinary restaurant guests. As a child,
she often went out to eat with her father. His standard line,
in Yiddish, was 'Nisht kein griner': anything but vegetables.
They frequented steakhouses, German schnitzel establishments, Chinese restaurants. These experiences shaped Mimi
Sheraton. She makes the price of the meal a regular element of
the *Times* restaurant review, something which has never been
done before. And she really does her research. When she decides
to write about sandwiches, she buys over a hundred in order
to compare them with academic precision. She doesn't want
to be recognized and given special treatment in the restaurants she reviews. So she wears wigs: black, silver-grey, red.[74]

And now, in 1977, the *New York Times* has sent her to
France for a whole month to research nouvelle cuisine. The
American gourmet press seems to have fallen for the newest
trend en masse. Sheraton isn't convinced. The Auberge de l'Ill
in Elsace and the Pic in Valence meet with her approval. But
the legendary tales of nouvelle cuisine? She is disappointed
and says as much in her review.

The trade's reaction is rich in nuance. Paul Bocuse attributes Sheraton's criticisms to sexual frustration. The Parisian

magazine *Metro* calls her a 'ketchup-slobbering Yankee'. She is referred to as 'Mimi Hilton' and 'Mimi Holiday Inn'. Eventually she appears on a French talk show, masked by a veil. For three whole hours, she debates with the stars of the world of French gastronomy. She tells Paul Bocuse that, in the interest of quality, he should perhaps start to spend some time in his restaurant's kitchen. When the show is over and the cameras are turned off, the gourmet chef becomes violent. He tries to rip off Sheraton's mask, she pushes him away, Bocuse stumbles and falls. Afterwards, Sheraton feels regret. That's what she tells *People* magazine. Regret that she didn't slap him in the face.[75]

*

In his autobiography Ray Kroc tells of innovation and creativity. He recounts how the Filet-O-Fish was founded in Cincinnati, Ohio, and the Big Mac in Pittsburgh. That the bag of French fries was too small for an innovator called Dave Wallerstein, a realization which, believe it or not, led to the creation of the big bag of fries. And how Herb Peterson, a resourceful contemporary from Santa Barbara, combined an egg, a slice of cheese, a slice of Canadian bacon and an English muffin, and in doing so laid the foundation stone for a product which, after three years of development in the company laboratories, was ready for market and christened the Egg McMuffin by a certain Patty Turner. All this wealth of invention, all of these achievements support Ray Kroc in his management of the McDonald's group.[76]

By this point, McDonald's has long since become an American institution. In 1980, there are 6,200 branches across the USA. And this is only the beginning. The fast-food industry is one of the most important sectors of the nation's economy.

Kroc doesn't agree with the term 'industry', however, because it implies commonalities between the gastronomic chains. He sees the competition differently. Kroc says: 'rat eats rat, dog eats dog'. His attitude is: 'I'll kill them before they kill me'. And so McDonald's advances into battle. Against Burger King, Burger Queen and Burger Chef. Against Red Barn, Hardee's, Jack in the Box and Carrol's. Against Kentucky Fried Chicken, Arby's, Pizza Hut, Taco Bell, Long John Silver's. Rat against rat.[77]

*

Chez Panisse is burning. It is a Saturday night, 7 March 1982, and Alice Waters is standing out on the street, separated from her restaurant by the fire department's cordons. Flames are lashing out from the top floor. Maybe she is even responsible for the fire herself, for the evening before she had been working at the grill. The cause will never be determined.

Her restaurant has managed to establish itself despite constant drug-taking amongst the workforce, and despite employees who see no problem in regularly making wine and food disappear. Business has been going well. The value of Chez Panisse has recently been estimated at $1.5 million. Craig Claiborne was there in 1981. He declared Alice Waters to be a 'chef of international repute', and described a pizza calzone from the Chez Panisse café as 'a triumph of taste and imagination'. A large New York publishing company is preparing the *Chez Panisse Menu Cookbook*, in which Alice Waters lays down her philosophy: the simplicity, the quality, the connection between the restaurant and her private kitchen. ('Sometimes', she writes dreamily, 'I may pull a bunch of thyme from my pocket and lay it on the table; then I wander about the kitchen gathering up all the wonderfully fresh ingredients I can find.'[78]). But now the restaurant is burning, and to Alice

Waters it feels as though her child is imprisoned inside the blaze. It is only a matter of minutes before the flames will engulf the weight-bearing columns of the wooden construction. If they do, the building will be completely destroyed.

Chez Panisse survives. And Alice Waters treats the fire as an opportunity to reinvent the restaurant. She realizes that its world is too narrow, based on too small a circle of people. She wants to open it up, for the people, for the customers. Because this is Berkeley, she finds intellectual assistance close by. She joins forces with Christopher Alexander, who has created a new architectural theory at the University of California. His work *A Pattern Language*, published just a few years before, leads architectonic achievement back to systemic connections, rather than independent strokes of genius. Alice Waters claims that the book becomes her bible.[79]

Alexander's urbanist manifesto calls for easily comprehensible entities, for openness: small shops, street cafés. His inspiration comes from shops in Moroccan, Indian and Peruvian towns, stores barely larger than 15 square metres. But a large beer hall is also part of his urban vision, a place where people can sing and shout, where they can 'cast off their worries' at long tables offering great freedom. Alexander's example: the Munich Hofbräuhaus.[80]

Based upon these principles, the renovation of Chez Panisse commences. Confronted with the fact that the wall between the kitchen and the dining room has been destroyed by the fire, Waters decides not to rebuild it. Just two weeks after the blaze, the restaurant reopens. The kitchen is refurbished, and no longer looks improvised but highly professional. Previously the white-uniformed chefs were hidden away. Now customers can watch them work.[81]

Here Waters veers away from Christopher Alexander's teachings. *A Pattern Language* recommends that one must maintain a 'balance' between too much enclosure and too much exposure. An individual engaged in his work should not be able to see more than four people at once from his workstation.[82] This certainly won't often be the case for the chefs of Chez Panisse.

*

Twelve-year-old Arlie is working as a waitress. In a sense. Her parents, diplomats, are giving a party, and Arlie is in charge of offering nibbles to the guests. The guests smile. But the smiles are more diplomatic than anything and don't look real, Arlie notices. She is used to talking to her parents about body language and its meanings, about handshakes and their duration, about averted gazes, stiff smiles, about the Bulgarian, Chinese or French ways of communicating. Even as a twelve-year-old, she is already beginning to ask herself whom she is dealing with when it comes to the smiling guests: actors who are only putting it on? Or people? And she wonders how to tell the difference between the person and the image he or she portrays.[83]

Arlie the twelve-year-old waitress grows up to become Arlie Hochschild, sociology professor, employed not far from Chez Panisse: at the University of California in Berkeley. In 1983, her book *The Managed Heart: Commercialization of Human Feeling* is published. The study is devoted to the questions which once played a big part in the lives of the Hochschild family. Now, though, the author applies them to modern capitalism. According to Hochschild, anyone who goes to work is compelled by their employer to friendliness, to restraint or even cheerfulness. Feelings are part of work and business life. Along with Goffman, she sees acting as part of everyday working life. But there's more to the story: a complex management of the everyday representation of emotions – by the employer and by individuals themselves.

What happens to the individual when serving others? Hochschild investigates a special type of restaurant: the flying kind. Amongst the stewardesses, she finds her most interesting subjects. 'Keep smiling' is a motto for all service-industry workers, but the flight attendants' training goes far beyond the compulsory smile. The women in uniform are expected to act as though their workplace is not, in fact, their workplace, but their private home. They are to treat the passengers not as customers, but as their personal guests. They are to make their customers' problems their own.[84] This requires not just the wearing of a smile, and superficial friendliness, but 'deep acting'. The flight attendants are to give themselves fully and completely to their role as friendly, attentive hosts. This, Hochschild demonstrates, has very real consequences. The employees' feelings no longer belong to them, but to the organization for which they work – to the extent that they no longer know how *they themselves* actually feel.

After the publication of her book, Arlie Hochschild is served with particular friendliness: on planes. Flight attendants recognize her everywhere she goes. Gratefully they squeeze her hand for giving their struggles a name, with her definition of 'emotional labour'. On two occasions, she receives a complimentary bottle of wine.[85] A television presenter who interviews her admits how much of an effort he has to make to put himself in the right mood for his work. Academics apply Hochschild's findings to studies of saleswomen, hairdressers, carers for the elderly. A new term for the worst-paid and hardest-working members of the service industry will come into being – a term Sartre, Orwell and Donovan didn't yet know. Waiters and waitresses, forced to smile, will soon belong to the 'emotional proletariat'.[86]

*

In 1984, the 'service/buffet' workers of the restaurant Waffenschmied will be declared the 'best collective in the socialist competition for the 3rd quarter'. Five years previously, Rolf Anschütz was permitted to leave the GDR for a four-week trip across Japan. Much to the joy of his hosts, he even ate live fish. A short while later, he receives the Hospitality in the Thüringen Forest diploma 'in recognition of exemplary achievements in gastronomic provision and care'. There is now a two-year wait for a table at the GDR's only Japanese restaurant. The restaurant collective has earned its accolades.

The restaurant also receives recognition from another source. Since the mid-1980s, the Stasi has recruited three informants from amongst the employees. In their efforts to grow the number to six, they try to enlist Anschütz's son as well, but he repeatedly refuses to collaborate.

In 1985, Anschütz's Far Eastern friends invite him back to Japan. This time, he will not travel alone: three of his chefs are permitted to accompany him. The GDR foreign ministry approves the trip and issues visas. But these never reach the gastronomes. After the fall of the wall in 1989, the documents are found unused in a safe. Irene Albrecht, communist bureaucrat who once criticized the Japanese bathing ceremony as 'poppycock', had confiscated the paperwork.[87]

Rolf Anschütz denies ever having collaborated with the Stasi. In 1986, he leaves the restaurant. Business continues without him. In the early 1990s, the restaurant's new owners will discover numerous hidden wires, leading to microphones set to record the dining-room conversations at Waffenschmied. The wires run together in the central office of communist Germany's most exotic restaurant.[88]

3

THE PRESENT DAY

H eston Blumenthal is eighteen years old and has a large pile of green beans in front of him. He has been instructed to cut off the ends, top and tail. He snips patiently and battles his way through the pile, only to find the next pile lying in wait. In his search for a chef apprenticeship, he wrote to twenty restaurants and received just one positive response: from Le Manoir aux Quat'Saisons, where he has been granted a one-week trial period.

The year 1983 is a good time to become a chef in England. Culinary interest is awakening. A new generation of chefs are about to break through. Raymond Blanc, who may soon be Heston's boss, is one of them. He is bringing nouvelle cuisine to Great Britain. His cooking is all about aesthetics and freshness, naturalness and purity.[1]

Bean-snipping Heston in Manoir aux Quat'Saisons is well prepared for this trial period. Perhaps too well. Two years ago, in Provence, his parents took him and his sister to one of the best restaurants in the world: the three-Michelin-star establishment L'Oustau de Baumanière. In Blumenthal's memory, this is where his life changed forever. Chirping cicadas, elegant waiters, thick linen serviettes, a wine menu as heavy as a stone tablet, the scent of lamb and lavender: a theatre for all the senses. Back in England, young Heston worked his way through the cookery book series *Les Recettes Originales* and used a dictionary to translate the top chefs' recipes. He is constantly reading the *Guide Michelin* and *Gault & Millau*. Since getting his driving licence, he regularly drives to a butcher's over twenty-five miles away to buy bones for stock. And he returns to his books again and again, the cookery books, the illustrated volumes showing the glamorous world of high-end gastronomy. Paul Bocuse, incensed by second-rate chicken; Alain Chapel, leaning over a plate in deep concentration. Heston studies the pictures and knows that he has found his true passion.

Now, in the kitchen of the excellent Raymond Blanc, Heston has his chance to become part of this world. He can finally make the transition from fantasy to reality. And so he snips his way through the second pile of beans, and the third pile, chops bucket load after bucket load of shallots, washes leeks, cleans fish, shells hazelnuts.

A week later, he gives up. This isn't how he imagined it.[2]

*

El Bulli, perhaps the most celebrated restaurant of the early twenty-first century, owes its existence to Margareta Schönova. In Prague, in 1945, she rescues a German soldier from becoming a Russian prisoner of war. Hans Schilling, her lover, is due to be transported, but Margareta supplies him with civilian clothing and enables him to escape. And marry her. They move to Gelsenkirchen, West Germany, where Hans starts a medical practice. Because business is going well, the Schillings are able to set off soon after the war to explore Europe in a camper van. In 1957, they find an enchanting piece of land on the Costa Brava and buy it for 15,000 pesetas. They want to build a medical establishment for senior citizens there, but don't receive the permit. Four years later, they have more success with a different idea: they set up a mini golf course.

Hans Schilling finds himself a younger woman, leaves his wife and rescuer and returns to Gelsenkirchen. Margareta Schilling, formerly of Prague, stays on the Catalonian beach and runs the bar attached to the mini golf course.

Hardly anyone is interested in playing mini golf. The property is too remote, the serpentine road which connects it to the nearest town too long. But the beach bar doesn't do too badly. Initially, Margareta just serves sandwiches and cold drinks. Soon she expands the menu, making gazpacho soup, fish and chicken. By 1964, the diner has been transformed into a grill restaurant. Before the lunchtime service, the kitchen staff walk down to the beach with menus and entice bathers up to the restaurant, where the guests use a hose to wash the salt water from their skin. They eat in their bathing suits. The diner used to be called Bar Alemany, but those times have passed. Margareta decides to hand the cooking over to others. And she renames the restaurant after her favourite breed of dog.[3]

*

Lake Fred and Lake Ed are the names of the two bodies of water on the Hamburger University campus. They were christened in honour of the former chairmen of the McDonald's group: Ed Rensi and Fred Turner. The university is in Oak Brook, a suburb of Chicago. The lecture rooms are painted bright green, a play on the maxim of the great Ray Kroc: 'When you're green, you're growing, when you're ripe, you rot.' A bust of the founder stands in the lobby. The professors at Hamburger University wear sports jackets emblazoned with the McDonald's logo. They offer courses such as Basic Operations, Intermediate Operations and Advanced

Operations. Anyone who successfully completes Advanced Operations earns a certificate declaring them to be a Doctor of Hamburgerology.

Robin Leidner is a graduate student at nearby Northwestern University. She is researching for her thesis, a sociological investigation of routinized work processes. She wants to find out how the McDonald's leadership of tomorrow is being trained. At first, the company is not very cooperative, but then she receives permission to enrol at Hamburger University. Now she can conduct her research without any limitations.

Students at Oak Brook have 'ketchup running in their veins'. They all live in a hotel at the edge of campus which exclusively houses McDonald's employees. Every morning, they walk over the bridge which stretches across Lake Fred. They often make comments like: 'We take hamburgers very seriously here.' They are guided by three core principles: quality, service and cleanliness. They attend lectures which go into the finest of details. The teaching staff occasionally go off-script in order to convey the material in a more lively fashion, but not too much. The programme provided by the internal Department for Syllabus Development is not to be meddled with. On their way to becoming Doctors of Hamburgerology, the students learn how to determine the precise temperature of deep frying fat, the exact consistency of milkshakes, the correct, uniform size of ice cubes. They try the Big Mac Special Sauce, compare it with gone-off Big Mac Special Sauce and learn to recognize the difference.[4]

*

Even after his return to Germany, Hans Schilling continues to play a part in business matters on the Costa Brava. In his quest to add a touch of gastronomic sophistication to the former beach bar – now called El Bulli – he straps a sorbet maker to the roof of his car and drives it all the way from Germany to the Mediterranean. It is one of the first sorbet makers in Spain. On the way, he stops off in Alsace at a restaurant which has just gone bankrupt, and buys their folk-costume style waiters' vests. They have V-necks and a green-red-brown-orange-blue flowery print. These, too, he delivers to El Bulli. Now the sorbet-serving waiting staff have rather a unique look. Schilling employs ambitious chefs: from Germany, Switzerland, Holland. Their model is French haute cuisine. The mini golf course is bulldozed, making space for the restaurant to expand.

In July 1975, *Gault & Millau* declares El Bulli to be 'la grande surprise de la Costa Brava'. The restaurant is part of a new, liberated Spain. After the death of Franco that same year, once-suppressed Catalan culture is being revived, and with it Catalan cooking. At El Bulli, this is combined – albeit carefully – with the principles of French nouvelle cuisine. The restaurant wins its first Michelin star, then a second. In the summer of 1983, a military service draftee called Fernando Adrià Acosta appears in the restaurant. He has no professional experience as a chef, but he works there for a few weeks on a trial basis. It is decided that he will be hired at El Bulli after his time in the military. He shows talent.[5]

*

Robin Leidner has made the transition from the theory of the Hamburger University into practice. She now works at a McDonald's restaurant near Chicago, in a branch more ele-gant than most. The franchise belongs to an expensive hotel and is furnished in art-deco style; it has no drive-through as it is mostly frequented by those on foot. The owner, his wife and their grown-up children look after the day-to-day matters, manage the employees and take care of the necessary renovations.

Down in the cellar, Robin and her new co-workers are watching a video. Smiling managers welcome them to the McDonald's family. The real-life manager is less friendly. He orders one worker not to wear her flashy earrings, and criticizes another for not wanting to work on Sundays because she is active in the church. All employees have to sign written agreements to take lie-detector tests.

Robin Leidner becomes a member of the French Fries Workgroup. They watch another video together. It presents the most important details: fries into the basket, basket into the deep fryer and out again, salt, bag up. There's nothing more to it. Up in the kitchen, Robin shadows an experienced colleague, and after one working day feels as though she can easily take on the tasks required of her.

Then, it's back down to the cellar. Another video explains the six-step process the Window Crew have to work through: greet the customer, take the order, assemble the order, present the order, take the money, thank the customer. An important detail: the paper bags in which the food and drinks are handed over to the customer must be folded twice at the top. This is essential, the trainer tells them, for leaving a professional impression.

The educational film informs the new workers of the standard phrases they are supposed to use to greet or say goodbye to the customer, or to encourage them to visit McDonald's again in the future. At the same time, however, they are told to vary these standard phrases. Robin Leidner has already learnt this at the Hamburger University: while McDonald's seeks to standardize all human interaction, part of this standardization includes the requirement that the clientele should not *feel* standardized. 'We don't want to create a conveyor belt atmosphere,' explains an instructor. 'Be enthusiastic and smile' is the most important guideline. Anyone who doesn't smile will be disciplined. But yet another rule instructs the workers to behave naturally, to be 'themselves'.[6]

*

The Schillings are retiring. In 1990, they offer to sell El Bulli to Juli Soler and Fernando Adrià Acosta, who jump at the opportunity. The new owners quickly win back the two Michelin stars which have been lost. The very same year, Soler is praised in *Gault & Millau* for his 'principles of modern cooking'. His business partner is not mentioned, neither by his Spanish nor his Catalan name. There is just a sweeping reference to the young chefs at El Bulli, who, according to *Gault & Millau,* combine regional traditions and modern cookery with 'intelligence and precision'.

And yet Adrià plays a very important role. The twenty-eight-year-old has already been head chef at the restaurant for three years. And he develops his personal signature. In a seemingly contradictory movement, he becomes an avant-gardist by turning away from the French avant-garde and integrating traditional Catalan cookery into his repertoire. He creates variations of garlic mayonnaise, chili pastes and fish stews. He works with ingredients usually untouched by haute cuisine: green olives and bacon, sardines and anchovies. In 1991, he decides to no longer serve tapas as aperitifs. The small plates are made into main courses. He takes inspiration from the bar snacks in his home town of Hospitalet, which are called *pica pica*. Adrià also turns his attention to desserts, and shadows the experts at a confectionery shop. The precision of the *pâtissier* impresses him, and this soon influences the whole kitchen at El Bulli. Stabilizers and emulsifiers are important to him, and are joined by confectionery terminology: the bonbon, the biscuit, the caramel.

There are hardly any customers in autumn and winter, so Juli Soler decides to open the restaurant for just seven months of the year. This gives Adrià the time to search for new inspiration. Economically, the early 1990s are an extremely difficult period. Adrià and Soler invest in further renovations, expanding the kitchen. But they are spending money they don't have. The majority of their clientele consists of German and French tourists. The customers they are trying to attract, gourmets from Barcelona, are sceptical about an establishment which is technically just a snack bar on the beach, hard to reach even by car and whose young head chef is reputed to be insane.

As is so often the case in restaurant history, a book saves the day. In 1993, *El Bulli: The Taste of the Mediterranean* is published. The cover reveals a new identity: the author of the cookbook, formerly known as Fernando, is now officially Ferran Adrià.[7]

*

Ildikó writes the inaugural menu on the chalkboard: veal shank with mashed potatoes and carrots, surprise dessert. At around 11.30 a.m., she sets up the board on the pavement in front of the restaurant. The Mondial is a family-owned business near Zurich: father and mother, two grown-up daughters, a few employees. Ildikó and her family are immigrants from Yugoslavia. 'We haven't got human status here yet,' says Ildikó's mother. 'We have to create it.' And Ildikó, her sister, mother and father are making every possible effort. During service, for example, the rule is: move quickly, but never run. Never go empty-handed, always carry something with you.

The aim is to reach the point where 'you're such a pro that no one even notices just how good you are'. Even when things are really hectic, they manage to serve the customers swiftly, but without rushing them. They are always ready with a compliment, perhaps commenting on the beauty of a lady's brooch. Ildikó cultivates perfectionism behind the counter too: at the coffee machine. The milk can't be too hot, otherwise it won't foam. The steam valve and liquid must be constantly in contact. Ildikó postpones her studies at the university – for the sake of the business, for the family. The construction workers are her favourite customers. They don't talk much and they know what they want: strong coffee. Ildikó's father does the cooking, even though he doesn't really know how. The mother is the go-to-girl for everything. Keeping the bathroom clean is at the top of her list. Again and again, she mops up the puddle of piss that regularly appears on the floor underneath the urinals.

It is the early 1990s, and the war in the now former Yugoslavia provides the background noise in Mondial. Out front, the xenophobic clientele talk about 'Albanians or people from some other country in the Balkans' and the fact that the '*homo balcanicus*' simply never went through the Enlightenment. Back in the kitchen, Dragana toils away. She had to leave her nine-year-old son behind in Sarajevo. She argues with the Croatian waitress Gloria about Tudjman, the Croat leader, but they're supposed to keep their voices down so the customers won't hear. When she's not peeling potatoes or cleaning carrots, Dragana takes the photo of her son from her bag and shows it around to the others. Over the preparation of cheese and ham toast and asparagus canapés, the topic of conversation in the kitchen is the extermination of an entire city. Corpses are being buried right next to the sites for the Sarajevo Winter Olympics.[8]

*

Robin Leidner shows that the routinized behaviour of the customers is just as important for McDonald's as the uniform work processes of its employees. Advertising, interior design and the example set by other customers ensure that visitors to each branch immediately make their way to the counter and order their food in the sequence desired by the company: first the burger, then the fries, and finally the drinks. The keys for desserts light up on the cash registers, prompting the staff to encourage customers to order something sweet to round off their meal. Any interruption to the standard communication process, whether it is provoked by a special request, an emotional outburst from a customer or a dispute over change, is to be handled not by the workers, but the branch managers.

The routines implemented by McDonald's apply to all involved parties. The consumers know very well that the friendly behaviour on the other side of the counter is just the product of training. And apparently one way to react to these emotional routines is to treat the smiling uniformed workers in as unfriendly a manner as possible. Some customers see this as a protest against the forms of commercialization practised by the hamburger chain.

There is another way of interpreting the routines. According to Robin Leidner, these schematic forms of interaction can also be perceived as authentic forms of social exchange. Their rules ensure a relatively minor loss of emotional energy. The routines make life easier for the men and women behind the counter. They feel protected by them. When they experience animosity and rejection by customers, they don't feel them as a personal rebuke, but a reaction to the mechanisms established by the company. And yet Robin Leidner's openness for the teachings of Hamburger University has its limits. She advises that civil, polite behaviour, and trust, integrity and personal freedom should also be adopted into the scripts that govern interactions: in fast-food branches and elsewhere.[9]

*

A shy customer tells Ildikó that something's wrong with her toilet. She tut-tuts at his shyness. And the turn of phrase. *My* toilet? Nonetheless, she goes to see what exactly is wrong with the men's bathroom. And she quickly finds out. The toilet lid is covered in shit and there's a pair of men's underpants on the floor. Someone has also smeared shit on the wall. She reaches for the rubber gloves which lie at the ready.

Six years ago, the local council for where they live outside Zurich voted on the naturalization of Ildikó's family. Now someone from the community has clearly decided to cover the Mondial bathroom in shit. Ildikó looks at the excrement on the wall. She can't make out any letters or symbols in the brown streaks. But, in her mind, she sees the town in all its neatness and wealth and xenophobia. She thinks of the slur 'Foreigner shits!' because that's the most common insult she hears. The 'friendly, respectable, controlled, politeness' now seems like 'a mask' to her. She imagines herself looking at the faces of the people in this community and asking: 'Who smeared shit all over our toilet?'

Later, she sits down with her parents to discuss the autumn menu. They have cleaned up the mess and the restaurant is closed for the night. Should they serve the red cabbage and *spätzle* with venison or deer? Wild boar, pears and cranberries, chestnuts? All Ildikó can think of is the shit over the wall and on the toilet seat, and the underpants on the floor. For her, this is the turning point. She'll leave the Mondial and this town. She'll move to the city, lead another life. But she hears her mother's voice in her mind: that here they can live in safety and that it's better than in Vojvodina, that immigrants cannot 'let everything get to them'. They have to play 'deaf' and 'dumb'. They have to be able to 'keep quiet' and 'put up with things', and only listen with 'one ear'. They have to assimilate. Her father says: in Yugoslavia, the only thing growing is the cemetery.[10]

*

Anthony Bourdain is working as a chef in Les Halles, a French brasserie in Manhattan. He has written two largely unsuccessful crime novels. Now he is trying his luck with an article exposing the secrets of the New York restaurant scene. He reveals that it is inadvisable to order fish on Mondays, when its freshness will be dubious. He informs diners that of course the bread they don't finish will be given to other customers and the uneaten butter will certainly make its way into the next hollandaise. And anyone who orders his steak well done, Bourdain warns, is sure to be served the worst, foulest-smelling, most gristly piece of meat to be found in the kitchen.

Bourdain's essay is also a declaration of love for restaurant life. He admires the teamwork. He describes chefs and their assistants as a collection of 'dysfunctional' outsiders. The professional kitchen is a gathering place for people with 'bad pasts': immigrants from all the countries you could possibly imagine, jammed together in the most cramped of spaces. Here the throwing of plates is considered a legitimate way to release frustration; hurling knives, on the other hand, is less widely accepted. Bourdain is no culinary genius, no Michelin-starred chef, but he is extremely proud of his work. This pride, though, doesn't prevent him from dreaming of a future as a writer.[11] And so he grafts away in the kitchen of Les Halles, hoping that someone will publish his essay.

*

The waitress in Mondial doesn't really exist. Ildikó is a character in a novel. She will only come to life in 2010, a creation of the Swiss author Melinda Nadj Abonji in her novel *Fly Away, Pigeon*. The restaurant is just one of its settings, although perhaps its most important. In Mondial, the rifts between the life experiences of different generations of immigrants come to the fore. Tolerant parents who are willing to assimilate work alongside their freedom-seeking children. The latter 'play' the waitresses, as though they are acting a part. They wear blouses which transform them into good daughters and bring the virtuous customers veal shank and coffee. And with her seemingly untidy narrative, the author, Melinda Nadj Abonji, who herself comes from this world, creates a stark contrast to the perfect service in the restaurant, to the smart blouses, to the silent wiping away of shit.

*

Cooking green beans is a nightmare at the Fat Duck. The gas pipelines are too narrow. Green vegetables have to be cooked in salted water, and because the flames are so weak they can only be cooked in small batches, each consisting of eight beans. One chef spends four hours dropping beans into the water and scooping them out again, then dropping new ones in and scooping them out again.

It was precisely this kind of monotony that once stopped Heston Blumenthal from making it past a week of learning the craft. Now it has caught up with him in his own restaurant kitchen. He needs the help of an expert: do green beans really have to be cooked in salted water? He contacts a chemical scientist: Peter Barham, University of Bristol. Barham is pleased when Blumenthal gets in touch. He explains to him that the chlorophyll in the beans is retained by magnesium, that the calcium in hard water drives out the magnesium and consequently the chlorophyll, the beans' green colouring. And that the salt works to prevent this. Which is exactly the kind of answer Blumenthal wants to hear.

Barham the scientist goes on to do a great deal more for Blumenthal. He puts him in touch with the company Firmenich, which develops aromas. Blumenthal travels to Switzerland and visits the company premises in a suburb of Geneva. He looks at numerous little bottles, each of them filled with an aroma, of boiled beef, for example, or the typical smell of a Chinese restaurant. The passionate scientists at Firmenich open Blumenthal's eyes, or rather his sense of taste and smell. And they, in turn, are curious to hear his ideas. He even gives a presentation at a small company symposium, for which he develops a gel from the aromas of basil, olive and onion. He gets to know more scientists, embarks upon collaborations. One day, Blumenthal notices that the taste of a tomato is more intense on the inside than out. Along with four co-authors, he publishes in the *Journal of Agricultural and Food Chemistry* an article entitled 'Differences in glutamic acid and 5'- ribonucleotide contents between flesh and pulp of tomatoes and the relationship with umami taste'. And he also solves the green bean problem. The next time the kitchen is renovated, Blumenthal has wider gas pipes put in.[12]

*

Shepherds are making their way over the plains of Causse de Larzac. It's a steppe-like world up here: sparsely populated, a karst plateau in the Massif Central. The sheep farmers are on their way to Millau, an almost 3,000-year-old town. They want to go to McDonald's. They are driving cars, forklifts and tractors. Some of them have brought chainsaws.

The burger chain branch they are heading towards is, at this moment in 1999, still under construction. But the sheep farmers don't want hamburgers or Chicken McNuggets; not now, not ever. They are protesting: against a special tax on the Roquefort cheese they produce, imposed by the US government because the European Union has declared an import ban on hormone-treated American beef. Former philosophy student José Bové leads the farmers towards the McDonald's. For him, the burger chain embodies the American attack on traditional forms of agriculture, nutrition and farming identity.

The convoy reaches the fast-food franchise. They announced their plans in advance, so the building site has been abandoned. More or less methodically, the farmers take the half-finished restaurant apart. Then they deposit the pieces of the McDonald's in front of the regional government building. To the crowd of onlookers in Millau, they hand out samples of their Roquefort cheese. Then they make their way back across town, break up the convoy and retreat to a local, non-American, restaurant to celebrate.[13] José Bové, who will soon become an EU Parliamentarian and a hero of the anti-globalization movement, spends nineteen days in jail because of this protest. He has shown himself unwilling to enter into any sort of settlement with the authorities. During this time of imprisonment, he loses 4 kilograms. That's how bad prison food is.

*

When they call him to the phone at Les Halles, Anthony Bourdain is in the middle of filleting a salmon. The chief editor of the *New Yorker* tells him he is going to print his manuscript. The essay is published in 1999, and from then on, Anthony Bourdain will no longer simply fillet fish. A publishing house swiftly offers him the opportunity of publishing his autobiography. Bourdain becomes one of the most well-known figures in American popular culture: bestselling author, television personality, critic, enfant terrible.

But first he has to actually write his life story. Early each morning, he sits down at his desk and thinks back over his career. He remembers the kitchen of the Rainbow Room in Manhattan, where one of his bosses continually grabbed his behind until Bourdain eventually rammed a meat fork into his hand. He studies the scars on his own hands, thinking of the stories they tell. Sometimes he also meditates on the food that defines the job, dreaming of sausages from Toulouse, duck confit, oysters. The most vibrant memories transport him back decades, to an Atlantic beach in Provincetown, and his first job as a chef. Here the waves crashed against the building and the kitchen staff behaved like pirates, grilling steaks and fish and swinging their knives. A wedding party, the bridegroom included, celebrated in the dining room while the bride had sex with one of the chefs behind the bins. According to Anthony Bourdain, witnessing this scene made professional cooking seem a particularly attractive career route.[14]

*

Barbara Ehrenreich is a feminist, biologist and investigative journalist, and she is sitting at a very expensive lunch in an American restaurant which professes to offer simple French country cuisine. She is here to discuss possible topics with an editor of *Harper's* magazine. She doesn't have any particularly concrete ideas yet. But the conversation is revolving around one of her favourite subject matters: poverty.

In the years leading up to this, Ehrenreich has written again and again about the most pressing social issues in the United States. She has a particular interest in poverty amongst those women forced into low-wage jobs in the 1990s as a result of cuts to social welfare services. She sees the United States as a nation shaped by social inequality, as a culture in which members of the upper classes profit from the fact that the working poor give them their underpaid work, sacrificing their health and strength in the process. To Ehrenreich, it is not the rich who are the true American philanthropists, but the poor, forced to subsidize the comfort of the middle classes.[15] And so she declares, at the table of this sophisticated yet supposedly very simple restaurant, that someone needs to write about precisely this topic. Old-fashioned journalism: someone must visit the places where the working poor toil away, and actually do the work themselves. Her editor looks at her and says just one word: 'You.'[16]

*

He is twenty-three years old when he forms his first band, in the autumn of 1971. It is to be named Blitzkrieg. At this point in time, just a quarter of a century after the end of the Second World War, this is perhaps a little too provocative a name for a German band. But this is exactly the point: he wants to break taboos. Unfortunately, there is already an English band called Blitzkrieg, so he decides instead on the name of a German field commander from the Thirty Years War. Now his band is called Wallenstein. They do well in France, where listeners appreciate the way their music unites melodies, brutality and sentimentality. Several albums are a flop, so they continue to experiment with new styles. Band members leave and new ones join. Drugs are always part of the picture. Finally, they find a marketable sound. Things go well at first: in 1979, their single 'Charline' climbs to number seventeen in the German charts. But then comes the era of the 'New German Wave', English-language lyrics are suddenly out of fashion, pop stars are wearing their hair differently. He has had enough. Project Wallenstein has reached the end of the road. Two decades later, he comes into the public view again, as a writer with the *Frankfurter Allgemeine Zeitung*. Jürgen Dollase, formerly of Wallenstein, now dedicates himself to culinary styles. And his opinions are firmly set.[17]

*

In the kitchen, a man is throwing frozen steaks at the wall and shouting: 'Fuck this shit!' And thus begins Barbara Ehrenreich's foray into poverty. She is working the afternoon and evening shifts as a waitress in a restaurant – which she calls Hearthside – in Southern Florida. Her hourly wage is $2.43. Tips are on top. The steak-thrower is the chef, Billy. He has just found out that his colleague on the morning shift didn't defrost the meat. Barbara is shown the ropes by the waitress Gail, whose boyfriend was murdered in prison a few months ago. Barbara Ehrenreich listens to the whole story, while simultaneously receiving an education in the basics of waitressing and the computerized till system.

Barbara learns, feels incompetent, learns more, and after a few days really starts to feel like a waitress. She puts this down to the 'service ethic' spreading out through her like a hormone. She wants to do her job right, even for $2.43 an hour. Her customers are construction workers, truck drivers, hotel staff. She wants to be polite to everyone. As often as possible, she offers refills of coffee and iced tea. She peps up the salads with a few fresh mushrooms. She even uses her rusty German to please a group of tourists with the question 'Ist alles gut?' For this, she receives a very generous tip, a rare occurrence amongst German customers. For a while, according to Ehrenreich, her stint as a member of the lower classes is a 'proletarian idyll'.

But there's a catch. This is an idyll that no one in modern-day America can survive in. Tips included, Barbara Ehrenreich earns around five dollars an hour. And she soon realizes that her colleagues aren't able to earn a living from their jobs at Hearthside either. Joan lives in a car which she has parked up behind a shopping centre. She showers at a girlfriend's house. Andy lives in a boat in a dry dock. Claude shares a one-bedroom flat with his girlfriend and two other housemates. None of them are able to rent their own apartment because none of them can afford to pay a month's rent upfront plus the standard security deposit of another month's rent on top. And so Barbara Ehrenreich has to take a second job in order to carry out her experiment with full realism. In the mornings, she waitresses at Jerry's, kitted out in a cheerful pink and orange Hawaiian shirt. In the afternoons, she works at Hearthside. She lasts two days.[18]

*

Sékou Siby's family have emigrated from Mali: to Abidjan in Ivory Coast. There are fourteen children, of which Sékou is the sixth. His father is a textile trader. His mother sells ice cream at a market stall. Sékou Siby is a gifted student. He studies hard and becomes a French teacher at a private school. The work is badly paid, and sometimes not paid at all. He takes part in labour disputes, but feels unsure of himself; he is always regarded as a foreigner from Mali rather than an Ivorian.

He manages to make his way to the United States on a tourist visa. There, he delivers goods for supermarkets. He is able to send a few hundred dollars a month back to his family in Abidjan. After only a year in New York, Sékou gets a new job, through a friend who is also from Ivory Coast. One of the best-known restaurants in the city is looking for a commis chef. Sékou gets the job, even though he has only ever cooked for himself.

He learns quickly in the kitchen, concentrating hard from his first day and constantly taking notes. Most of the cooks above him are from Central and South America. He can speak and understand Spanish, so he listens to them, writes down their secrets and recipes. After six months, he is promoted. Now he is a real chef, part of the team, in the kitchen and outside it. The Mexican cooks and *pâtissiers* invite him to join their football team, which meets in Corona Park in Queens. In 2001, Sékou Siby has arrived at last, at the Windows on the World restaurant in the World Trade Center.[19]

*

Barbara Ehrenreich is now living in trailer number 46 in the Overseas Trailer Park. She didn't last long waitressing both mornings and afternoons. So she has switched her waitress job in Hearthside for one as a maid in the hotel next to Jerry's, and switched her morning shift at Jerry's for the lunch shift. But that's not really working out either. One of the other maids warns her that she's too old for this kind of strain. It has to work, though, because otherwise she won't have enough money. There are 8 million Americans, more than 6 per cent of those in employment, who have two jobs. So why shouldn't she be able to handle it?

After the end of her shift in the hotel there is just enough time for what Ehrenreich, inspired by Karl Marx, calls the 'Reproduction of Labour Power'. She takes four pills for the backache she's developed from making beds and cleaning. She showers quickly. She wipes the most obvious salad dressing and ketchup stains from her Jerry's work trousers, pulls on her cheerful Jerry's Hawaiian shirt, eats a few chicken nuggets and goes to work.

At Jerry's, the spray-cream canisters have recently been switched for bags of ready whipped cream, because the workers were using the propellant from the canisters to get high. Today, a cook called Jesus is manning the kitchen. He is pretty much a beginner. Tables 24, 25, 27 and 28 become occupied at the same time. This is Barbara Ehrenreich's area. She sees that there are ten English tourists at table 24, and four yuppie types at table 28. The Brits order all kinds of drinks: one orders beer and water with a slice of lemon, another orders a milkshake and an iced tea. The couple at 25 complain that the iced tea isn't fresh enough and that the table is sticky. The United Kingdom at table 24 orders numerous dishes: from mozzarella sticks, banana splits and diverse breakfast specials to chicken strips, which are actually supposed to be appetizers, but end up coming at the same time as everything else, with the result that everything else has to go back again so that the chicken strips really can be appetizers. Barbara Ehrenreich has carried everything across to the table already, three journeys with three trays, and now brings everything back again to Jesus in the kitchen and to the microwave. All the tables in the restaurant are occupied and Jesus can't keep up. Barbara carries the main courses back over to table 24. Great Britain rejects the warmed-up dishes for not being hot enough, and Barbara, dog-tired from making beds and cleaning bathrooms all morning, transports them back again, burgers, eggs, toast, sausages, three trays, three journeys, and now she no longer has any idea who at table 24 actually ordered what and what precisely the difference is between the breakfast specials, in other words between a 'traditional', a 'super scramble' and an 'eye-opener', and her colleague Joy is yelling at her, telling her she should know that already. And while Joy is yelling at her about the 'super scramble' and the 'eye-opener', a customer, albeit not one from tables 24, 25, 27 or 28, appears in the kitchen and shouts that he's been waiting for his food for twenty-five minutes, upon which Joy, the shift supervisor at Jerry's who has just finished yelling at the prominent writer Barbara Ehrenreich, barks at the customer that he should kindly remove himself from the kitchen, then throws a tray at the young, bungling chef Jesus. This scene will stay in Barbara's memory as her last from Jerry's, because she leaves. Just like that. She doesn't hand in her notice, or take the wages due to her. She doesn't ask anyone's permission. She just keeps walking. Out of the door and into the parking lot.

Barbara Ehrenreich, doctor of biology, embarked upon this waitressing job as an academic experiment. In the end it turned out to be not an experiment for other people, but a test for her. And she didn't pass. Outside, she realizes that she hasn't shared her tip money, as agreed, with her genuinely poor colleagues, those who can't just go back to an upper-middle-class existence in which the $30 they have to pay out of their own pocket for khaki-coloured Jerry's work trousers doesn't have an impact for weeks on end. This realization pains Barbara Ehrenreich. She doesn't cry, as she writes later in her successful book *Nickel and Dimed: On (Not) Getting by in America*. But there was nothing triumphant about her departure from Jerry's, no cathartic 'Fuck you' outburst. Just the feeling of having failed.[20]

*

For the past year or so, Jürgen Dollase has been working as a restaurant critic for the *Frankfurter Allgemeine Zeitung*. He has written an essay, which, in the style of Adorno's *Introduction to the Sociology of Music*, categorizes specific types of consumers in advanced gastronomy. He has eaten at Alain Ducasse's three-Michelin-star establishment in Paris. He praised the gourmet chef for his sweetbreads, but condemned him for his 'crispy farmhouse bacon with caramelized potatoes, truffled salad of pig's head with bitter herbs' (Dollase: 'A horrendous dish'). He also got worked up about the 'chain-smoking Japanese in casualwear' at Ducasse's tables and about the American businessman – 'with a very blonde, backcombed companion' – who would eat nothing but meat. At the turn of the millennium, he tried the New Year's menus of Germany's top chefs and found Johann Lafer's Angus beef tenderloin with a kaffir-lime crust, sweetheart cabbage-chili strudel and plum wine sauce to be the 'most entertaining' amongst the millennial delicacies on offer.

Now, in October of the year 2000, he feels that the time has come to read the riot act to food criticism in its current form. He attacks the 'generosity' of German restaurant critics, as well as their tendency to 'personalize' their evaluations and, above all, 'burden the groundless framework' of their judgements with 'anecdotes and affectations from their youth'. The critics have grown old, says Dollase. The focus on 'the refinement of the familiar' is no longer appropriate, he says. Gourmet cuisine is not the 'natural enhancement' of 'home cooking'. Dollase demands 'greater analytical precision', more 'transparency', a 'stylistic classification' and the 'consistent use of a catalogue of criteria which is conveyed in as precise a manner as possible'. He admonishes: 'The damage which can be unleashed by indifferent praise is largely overlooked.'

In spring of 2001, Johann Lafer finds out first hand what this means. A year before, the television chef was praised by Dollase for being 'entertaining'. But this is not enough to save him. Dollase eats at Val d'Or in Stromberg and is underwhelmed. He declares Lafer's quails to be undercooked and devoid of flavour. The potatoes are 'cold and stale'. He tastes veal fillet which seems 'denatured'. He encounters a 'horrifically salty' polenta. For dessert, he tries a champagne mousse with a 'slightly dried out gelée covering'. In summary, Dollase declares that a 'certain unfreshness' is the signature of Lafer's creations. He even injects an element of pathos: it was 'the people' who made the television chef Johann Lafer 'great'. And now the people should get something in return. Jürgen Dollase, formerly of Blitzkrieg, formerly of Wallenstein, knows exactly what it is that Johann Lafer owes the people: 'more precision'.[21]

*

On 11 September 2001, seventy-three Windows on the World employees lose their lives. The victims are kitchen workers towards the lower end of the hierarchy, who were in the process of preparing a large breakfast party. Sékou Siby is off work on this day. He has swapped his Tuesday shift with his colleague Moises Rivas, who does not survive the terrorist attack on the Twin Towers.[22]

In autumn 2001, the former employees of Windows on the World try to find new jobs. Most of them are immigrants. David Emil, the owner of the destroyed establishment, initially announces that he will take all of them with him to his new enterprise Noche. But he doesn't keep his promise, taking just a few. Sékou Siby is so traumatized by the catastrophe that he no longer wants to work in the restaurant business. He becomes a taxi driver. His former colleagues, meanwhile, get to know the scandalous side of the New York gastronomy industry. In the World Trade Center they were unionized, receiving above average salaries and benefits. These are not on offer elsewhere. It is possible to make a living from only one in five jobs in the American food industry. Most employees are dependent on tips. For immigrants without papers, who make up roughly 40 per cent of all restaurant workers, the situation is even more precarious. They are incredibly vulnerable to exploitation, because any conflict with their employers could lead to their being reported to the authorities.

*

Kurdish Mehmet Turgut, born in 1979, grows up in Kayalik Köyü, a mountain village in eastern Turkey. There are very few economic prospects in the region. When he is fifteen, Mehmet and his older brother Yunus exchange passports so that Mehmet can avoid military service. That same year, hidden in a lorry, he sets off en route to Germany. He has friends and relatives there. But his request for asylum is rejected, because persecution of Kurds by the Turkish government is not accepted as a valid reason. And so, at the age of seventeen, Mehmet Turgut is deported back to Turkey. Two years later he returns to Germany, lodges another asylum application, and receives word he is to be deported again. He goes underground for a while, but is ultimately deported, before returning once more to Germany with the help of people smugglers. Again he is arrested, then released, pending renewed deportation. By this point – Mehmet Turgut is twenty-six years old now – an acquaintance called Haydar Aydin, also from Kayalik Köyü, gives him the opportunity to work at a food stand. The stand is called Mr Kebab Grill. It is located in the north-east of Germany, in Rostock-Toitenwinkel, amidst socialist high-rise apartment buildings and detached houses. Mehmet stays with Haydar Aydin. But he can't shake his anxiety. Every day, he fears being imprisoned and deported.[23]

*

Saru Jayaraman, a Yale-educated lawyer, is twenty-seven. She knows restaurants only from the perspective of being a customer. Nonetheless, in 2001 she takes over a new sub-department of the Hotel Employees and Restaurant Employees Union: the Restaurant Opportunities Center. Her first task is to organize the former employees of Windows on the World. The first direct action is against Noche. On the restaurant's opening night, when the socialites make their way along the red carpet in Times Square, they are met by unemployed waiters and cooks. The *New York Times* picks up on the story of the broken promise. Just a few days later, the owner agrees to a meeting with Jayaraman and backs down: he will employ more of his former staff.

This is the Restaurant Opportunities Center's first success. But Saru Jayaraman has bigger plans. She becomes one of the leading minds of a movement which aims to fight the harsh exploitation rife in the restaurant industry. Seven years after the catastrophe of September 11, Jayaraman takes over the national leadership of the Restaurant Opportunities Center. And the new leader of its New York branch is Sékou Siby, erstwhile French teacher, then cook, then taxi driver, now union official.[24]

*

Bill is standing at the grill in Mario Batali's Babbo. He is not a qualified cook, but he loves the work. There are two kinds of cooks, says Bill: those who bake, working in a more scientific way, with precision, measuring the ingredients exactly – and those who cook meat. This kind of cook doesn't measure, but feels. No textbook can teach you that. How does a cook know when the lamb is medium rare? Because of the way it gives when you touch it, a pillow-like feel, a bit like the softest point of Mario Batali's hand, which doesn't help Bill much initially, because his hands are different from Mario's.

Batali is a television chef with his own show, *Molto Mario*, known across America, the kind of guy everyone likes, both machos and intellectuals. And for the last few weeks, Bill has been working for him in his New York restaurant. Even better than that: now he's working the grill, at the heart of the action. Bill grills the meat for all of Babbo's meat-eating customers. In order to learn this 'feeling' for himself, in order to become a real meat chef at the grill, he has begun to feel the meat not to check whether it's ready, but to check whether it's not ready yet. Touch, not ready, touch, still not ready, touch, not quite, touch, ready. He loves this way of learning. It is childlike, completely different from that of the world he grew up in, and to the desk work he did before. Here, in the kitchen, it's all about the body, about the senses, about what you smell, shape and feel.

Bill at the grill both loves and hates the evenings, when Babbo is almost unbearably hectic. A new order comes every few seconds. Lamb, lamb, ribeye steak, more lamb, lamb, rabbit, more lamb, sometimes medium, sometimes well done. Get out the meat, season, grill, feel, grill, feel, get out the meat, season, grill, more lamb, lamb, rabbit, lamb. Flames lick from the grill, not a good thing, there's too much meat, too much fat, so Bill grills around the flames. He sweats, feels the panic that he can't keep up, feels the adrenaline enabling him to keep going regardless, hears the voice of his colleague, telling him that this is the 'buzz' they live for. The heat. The hectic pace. The energy the civilians out there will never feel. He, Bill, is at the heart of this energy. At least until Batali comes back and notices what's going wrong.[25]

*

Ismail Yaşar runs a kebab stand opposite a Nuremberg school. Yaşar was born in Alanyurt in Turkey and came to Germany in 1978. He was granted asylum. He is fifty years old, on his third marriage, and a welder by trade, but for the last ten years he has run various doner kebab stands in Nuremberg. This one is his own. His son Kerem attends the school across the street. The stand is in a simple white container next to a supermarket. The kebabs cost two euros each. Ismail Yaşar sometimes gives Kerem's schoolmates free ice lollies. In the evenings, he sits next to the container, drinking tea with acquaintances from the neighbourhood.[26]

*

Head chef Mario has been off travelling on a promotional tour for the last month. Now he is back. And he's taking a closer look at Bill's work. He feels one of Bill's grilled pork loins. It isn't properly cooked through yet. Off to the salamander with it; it might be salvageable still. Then he turns his attention to Bill's rabbit. He inspects it with his fingers. Overcooked. There's nothing that can be done. The rabbit is served regardless. Mario turns his back to Bill. He has a short discussion with two of the other cooks. Bill can't make out what they're saying, but he does hear the word 'unacceptable'. Someone else takes over at the grill. Bill has nothing to do. He stands in the cramped kitchen, trying not to get in anyone's way. He waits. No one looks at him. After an hour, once Mario Batali has gone home, one of the chefs takes pity on Bill and lets him go back to the grill.[27]

*

Heston Blumenthal is flying to Madrid. First class, for the first time in his life. He is picked up from the airport in a luxury BMW and taken to a luxury hotel. Everything around him is mahogany and marble. In Palacio Municipal, hundreds of people are waiting for him. They are the attendees of Fusion II, a spectacular gastronomic conference held in January 2004. The best chefs in the world are gathered here: Frédy Girardet, the Troisgros brothers, Ferran Adrià, Juan Mari Arzak. Simultaneous interpretation is offered via headsets. Gigantic projection screens show the speakers and their presentations.

At home in England, Blumenthal's restaurant is on the verge of bankruptcy. The Fat Duck's two Michelin stars are no guarantee of commercial success. Ambitious dishes like Salmon in Liquorice Gel are not exactly customer magnets. On Saturdays and Sundays, most of the tables are booked. But during the week, the restaurant is practically empty. Sometimes Blumenthal's team only serve two tables a night, and on one occasion there are just six diners. Blumenthal doesn't know how he's going to keep paying his staff.

On each seat in the lecture hall in Madrid, Heston has left an envelope with the Fat Duck logo. It contains, amongst other things, a balloon with benzaldehyde, the aroma substance of marzipan. He has ten minutes for his presentation. Before the greats of the culinary world, he speaks about his cooking techniques. He shows how to use liquid nitrogen. He talks about the pump with which he makes gelatinized quail consommé. And once Blumenthal's ten minutes are up, the almost bankrupt gastronome asks the guests to pick up the balloons. They, the most talented chefs on the planet, blow them up and let them float away. The balloons circle and spiral wildly around the hall. And a cloud of marzipan aroma rises up, filling the entire auditorium.

*

On the morning of 25 February 2004, Mehmet Turgut turns on the kebab skewer, puts on the coffee and slices vegetables. At around 10.20 a.m., Haydar Aydin finds him. Mehmet Turgut has taken shots to the temple, the right side of his neck and the back of his neck. He dies in the ambulance. On the morning of 9 June 2005, shortly before 9 a.m., Ismail Yaşar receives a delivery of flatbreads. Shortly before 10 a.m., a customer orders a kebab. At 10.15 a.m., Ismail is found dead at his food stand. He has been shot in the upper body and the head. As well as Mehmet Turgut and Ismail Yaşar, a florist, a tailor, a locksmith's assistant, two fruit and vegetable traders, a kiosk manager and an internet café manager are murdered in German cities between 2000 and 2006. Almost all the victims are originally from or have family roots in Turkey, while the locksmith's assistant Theodoros Boulgarides was from Greece. In the media, the term 'Kebab Murders' is established in connection with this series of attacks. Only in the Turkish-language press does the term 'donerci cinayetleri' (Kebab Vendor Murders) draw attention to the fact that the victims of the attacks are human beings.[28]

Fingerprints and DNA tests are taken from fifteen-year-old Kerem, Ismail Yaşar's grieving son. He is suspected of having murdered his father. Next, the prosecutors speculate that Ismail Yaşar was dealing drugs from his stand. They inspect the kebab skewer for traces of narcotics. For months on end, the establishment is sealed up. But Kerem's mother has to keep paying the rent, and subsequently gets into debt.[29]

Bosporus, the Nuremberg police special unit set up to investigate the crimes, eventually takes another step: they open a kebab stand, where undercover investigators prepare Turkish specialities. Suppliers' invoices are intentionally left unpaid: the fast-food stand's debts end up running to 30,000 euros. This is an attempt to lure in the murderers of individuals like Mehmet Turgut and Ismail Yaşar, whom the special unit now suspect to be part of a Turkish organized crime ring.

Armed debt collectors fail to materialize. Only one noticeable incident is recorded: a middle-aged man appears in front of the kebab stand, shouting abuse. He complains about the fact that the Turks are 'taking jobs away from the Germans', that they are 'spreading out all over Germany'. As he curses, he points at the wanted poster which refers to the series of murders of Turkish small business owners and announces that if the Turks refuse to be got rid of by other means, then this is 'how they'll have to be sent home'.[30]

*

The top chefs gathered in Madrid are delighted. Heston Blumenthal has arrived in the world he dreamt of as a young boy. But what saves the Fat Duck is neither the marzipan cloud nor the impressive pump technique used to produce the quail consommé. While he is still in Madrid, Blumenthal finds out he is to receive his third Michelin star. Journalists besiege him. He knows the award will pull him out of his financial crisis, as the third star makes the Fat Duck one of the best restaurants in the world. Back in England, now part of the international elite of gourmet chefs, he will have new problems to solve. How to develop his cooking so that he can hang on to the third star, for example. And what to do when a customer who wants to dine at the restaurant asks where he can land his helicopter.[31]

*

Bill from the grill at Babbo, Bill Buford, is a 'word guy'. That's how he refers to himself. He's not really a cook, but an editor at the *New Yorker*. He categorizes himself as one of those typical big-city types for whom life revolves around language, reading, abstraction, deductive thinking. Now he wants to get to know a different, more organic form of knowledge. He wants 'simple pleasure'. For him, cooking is the only activity which allows him to experience elementary joy and somatic learning. That's why he is trying his hand at the grill in Babbo, with varying degrees of success. That's why he learns how to mould pasta dough into the shape of a little ear with the help of his thumb and a piece of wood. He botches several of his first attempts, then eventually gets the hang of it and subsequently produces hundreds and thousands of orecchiette, each one a work of art. Bill Buford wants to possess 'kitchen awareness'. He wants to learn not from books, but with his body; how to wield the knife in order to debone lamb, how to bind together pieces of meat, caramelize vegetables, spray droplets of sauce on a plate, how to shake the frying pan in such a way that all the contents are flipped in one go and how to jiggle it so that just the contents at the edge turn over.[32] His search for this state of awareness has led him to Mario Batali, and next he will implement what he has learnt in Italy, where he becomes the apprentice of a traditional butcher.

At the end of this journey, Bill Buford, as much of a 'word guy' as before, formulates a clear theory of knowledge and life. Hands are the most important part of this concept: the hands of cooks and other manual workers who are involved with food. Sometimes, says Buford, these people make their hands small. Sometimes they make them big. They roll out pastry, they work meat with their knives. And in doing so, they don't just supply people with food, but also provide current generations with knowledge about how their parents and their grandparents worked with their hands

In today's world, says Bill Buford, making food with one's hands is an act of protest. He shows that these traditions, thousands of years old, are in danger. Nowadays no one pays any attention to the cooks' hands, which act both as an instrument of self-expression and as a reminder of the ancestors who shaped who we are now. For Buford, it is not fast food which is responsible for destroying these traditions. It is the fact that the consumer now defines what there should be to eat and when – and no longer the producer, the cook, who knows what is to hand and what is not.[33]

*

Rose petals taste like artichokes: or at least the cooked petals from imported Ecuadorian eco-roses do. That's the idea behind this dish. The rose petals are blanched and refreshed in iced water, then arranged on the plate in the shape of a rose. The dish looks and smells like a rose made from finely cut artichoke leaves. But in fact it really is a rose, made from rose petals which look like artichoke leaves. That's the point.

The following idea is similar: lentils for a lentil soup are, in actual fact, not lentils, but instead lentil-like creations made from a dough of melted butter and sesame paste. The dough is passed through a delicate syringe. The lentils which aren't lentils are served in a small glass bowl, in a clear broth, with a few herbs. It is a reference to traditional lentil soup. Except that these lentils aren't lentils, just as the roses aren't artichokes. And there's more: anyone with the cliché of so-called 'molecular cooking' in their mind who recognizes the lentils as not-lentils and suspects they have been treated with secret chemical additives would be wrong. Nothing but butter and sesame paste has been used. And iced water.

This is 'techno-emotional cuisine', as Ferran Adrià calls it. With ironic dishes such as these, El Bulli has become part of the global art and culture scene. Plates, bowls and cutlery from El Bulli are exhibited in the Pompidou Centre in Paris. International documentary film-makers shoot in the restaurant. Adrià is invited to Documenta 12 as an artist. During the hundred-day-long art exhibition, two other Documenta guests, selected by the curators, visit El Bulli each day and dine there.[34] By mid-2007, there are over 2,500 articles reviewing or discussing the establishment in the restaurant archive: 14,000 pages in total.[35]

In the international press at this time, the IAAEBP emerges to delight and beguile readers. The abbreviation (which stands for the 'I ate at El Bulli piece') represents the format of an enthusiastic and detailed journalistic report on culinary experiences in Adrià's restaurant. Key ingredients of the IAAEBP are the perilous journey over the narrow serpentine road, meditations on the olive, and religious or sexual undertones in the menu.[36] There is much less frequent mention of who actually produces this menu and how: the lentils which aren't lentils and the rose-artichoke-rose.

*

Juan Moreno can't help but gag at the smell of refuse. Marabou storks – dark, carcass-eating birds – hover above him. Like vultures, only bigger, notes Moreno. He is a German journalist and he is walking across a landfill site in Nairobi. A man called Safari-Safari is leading him and the photographer Mirco Taliercio over the Dandora landfill site. It spans 40 hectares, and the mountains of waste are 30 metres high. Juan Moreno is thankful for the wind, which is blowing some of the stench away from them. Smoke rises up from burning rubber on the piles of waste, and even this is more pleasant than the stench of the rubbish. Safari-Safari moves quickly and deftly through the mountains of garbage, the fires, the black clouds, and the numerous women who are searching through the rubbish with their bare hands for items of value.

Moreno and Taliercio are trudging over the landfill as part of a book they are working on about chefs. 'They tell the best stories,' says Moreno. The author and photographer undertake long journeys. They visit the Madrid restaurant which has a monopoly on the production of Spanish bull's tail and stores more than a thousand vacuum-packed portions in a deep freezer in the cellar. They record the recipe for the bull's tail soup: three onions, ten mushrooms, four carrots, 150 grams of herbs, half a litre of strong red wine, three and a half hours cooking time. Moreno and Taliercio visit Nurse Tifa: a cook from Portland, Oregon, with an extremely high number of internet views, renowned for producing cooking videos half-naked. Their conversation with her revolves less around the food and more around the size and disputed naturalness of her breasts. Here in Nairobi, the reporters are looking for a restaurant run by a woman named Faith

Muthoni. According to Safari-Safari, they will find it behind the next hill of waste.[37]

*

In the kitchen at El Bulli, the preparation process for the rose petals takes two hours. Rose petals into the boiling water. Rose petals out of the boiling water. Rose petals into the iced water. Rose petals out of the iced water. Repeat. Repeat. Once this procedure finishes, the next begins. The rose petals are rolled out and laid flat. The lower end of each rose petal must be lifted up a little for visual effect. Once they are dried out, they are placed on the plate shortly before being served. Each season, thirty-two unpaid young cooks work in El Bulli. Ten of these *stagiaires* spend an hour each day laying rose petals on plates. The outer circle, the middle circle, the inner circle.

In order to make the lentils which aren't lentils, eight *stagiaires* have to push 2,000 lentil drops through syringes into iced water each day. It sounds simple enough: put a little of the batter into the syringe, push, and done. But each single cook spends more than an hour on his 250 lentils. Because there is no way of speeding up the process. Because even just a little extra pressure on the syringe will result in the production of not lentil-like drops, but unusable worms. The batter can't be too cold, either. So it has to be warmed up again and again throughout the process. Hands and arms cramp up from the extremely precise manner of holding the syringe. And the worst part of the job: the young women and men are constantly aware of how much batter – so much batter! – is still in the bowl. It's always more than they think.

This is how things are done at El Bulli, the former beach bar. And Lisa Abend, an American journalist, knows all this, because instead of composing an IAAEBP, she spends an entire season, with the full support of Ferran Adrià, shadowing the work in the kitchen of what is reputed to be the most creative restaurant in the world. Lisa Abend learns that monotony is the true secret to Adrià's success. Dozens of young men and women make lentil drops, lift rose petals out of the water and lower them back in. At the end of the day, they are learning nothing from these tasks. No other kitchen in the world has the resources to spend hours of work time creating rose-artichoke-roses. And no one grows as a chef by pushing 250 sesame-paste-butter-lentils through a syringe with exactly the right amount of pressure. And yet Ferran Adrià is drowning in job applications.[38]

*

Mustafa Turgut can no longer bear it in Kayalik Köyü. There are too many rumours circulating since his older brother was shot in Germany. The German police interrogate family members, assuming it was a revenge killing. In doing so, they only intensify the rumours. Haydar Aydin, owner of the Mr Kebab Grill in Rostock, brought Mehmet's body back to Kayalik Köyü. He too is a suspect, though not in the eyes of Mehmet's family, who are convinced that German neo-Nazis murdered him. The parents are isolated in the village. They haven't only lost a son, says Mustafa Turgut later, but also 'their home, friends and relatives'.

Mustafa sets off for Antalya, a seaside resort on the south coast. He finds work as a waiter in a restaurant there. He too believes that Germans murdered his brother. But when he serves tourists from Germany in the restaurant, they make a different impression. They seem polite and nice. Customers from other countries leave rubbish lying on the tables, but the Germans, at least the ones Mustafa encounters here, are different. They clean up after themselves, even brushing away the crumbs on the table. They treat him, their waiter, with respect.

In November 2011, Mustafa Turgut's cousin calls him from Germany. He tells him that it has now been established who killed Mehmet: German neo-Nazis – just as the Turguts always suspected. In spring of 2013, Mustafa will travel to Munich to appear as a joint plaintiff in the so-called NSU Trial, shedding light on the murder spree. He will receive a work permit and a job in a restaurant, just as his older brother did before him. He will be twenty-two years old by that point, and when asked to comment on his relationship with German people he will say: 'A country is like a hand. Every finger is different.'[39]

*

In the autumn of 2012, the academic journal *Epidemiology and Infection* accepts a paper by the authors Smith, McCarthy, Saldana, Ihekweazu, McPhedran, Adank, Iturriza-Gómara, Bickler and O'Moore. The topic is a Norovirus outbreak in an English restaurant in January and February of 2009. The nine authors, between them, work across four different areas of the British health authority. They focus their attentions on the over 200 people who became infected with the pathogen in the same restaurant, having surveyed 591 people. Of these, 386, with an average age of thirty-eight, returned their completed questionnaires. And 240 claim to have displayed the symptoms of the virus: 82 per cent had diarrhoea, 78 per cent felt nauseous, 73 per cent vomited, 65 per cent had stomach pains. The symptoms lasted for three days. The researchers also collected stool samples, from the guests as well as from the restaurant staff.

The authors from the Health Protection Agency prove, first, that oysters served in the restaurant were contaminated with the Norovirus. Shell-like organisms, they show, are often contaminated when human excrement pollutes the seawater in which they are bred. Second, the authors prove that there were hygiene issues in the restaurant itself. Employees reported that they turned up to work despite having symptoms of illness. The researchers also suspect that food items in this particular kitchen are handled in a very complex and protracted manner, and that there were therefore several opportunities for the virus to be transferred from infected cooks to the dishes. In addition, they report that the health authorities were informed very late and that this accelerated the outbreak of the epidemic.

By this time, Heston Blumenthal is a household name. British television viewers know him from the television series *Kitchen Chemistry with Heston Blumenthal*, from *Heston Blumenthal: In Search of Perfection* and from *Heston Blumenthal: Further Adventures in Search of Perfection*. They know the shows *Heston's Feasts*, they know *Heston's Mission Impossible* and *How to Cook Like Heston*, as well as *Heston's Fantastical Food* and *Heston's Great British Food*. Between 2005 and 2011, he publishes seven books. He has two honorary degrees and an honorary Masters, is the first chef to be awarded an Honorary Fellowship by the Royal Society of Chemistry, and is presented with an Order of the British Empire for his services to the connection between science and the culinary arts.

Blumenthal's appearance on the pages of *Epidemiology and Infection* is less prominent. The authors matter-of-factly point out that the establishment they analysed 'uses an approach based on the principles of molecular gastronomy'. They explain that the restaurant 'prepares and serves unusual dishes using what it describes as innovative methods'. Attentive readers of the essay will recognize the Norovirus-contaminated dish from the pages of Heston Blumenthal's *Fat Duck Cookbook*: oyster with passion fruit jelly and lavender. This sophisticated creation served at the Fat Duck unleashed one of the worst cases of food poisoning in recent British history.[40]

*

Faith Muthoni's restaurant is constructed from branches and tarpaulin. The pots rest over a log fire. She always cooks the same dish, which consists of rice, beans and cornflour, and serves it on plastic plates salvaged from the landfill. The price for one portion is twenty cents, when converted into euros. She uses no seasoning and only the cheapest beans. She sells the food to people who come to the landfill each day.

Faith Muthoni lives right next to the dump. She is a single mother of five children. The heavy metal content of the landfill causes cancer, skin diseases, anemia. The mercury pollution is twenty-six times higher than the limit established by the UN's environmental programme. The iron content is twenty-seven times higher. Each day, Faith Muthoni cooks from nine in the morning until five in the afternoon. She has one day off a week. Sometimes she sells just fifteen meals a day, sometimes, on very good days, forty. A violent religious sect has the landfill site in its grips, demanding protection money, ruling over everyday life.

Mirco Taliercio photographs Faith Muthoni on the land-fill site. In the picture, she is carrying a child on one arm. An older child stands before her. No one is smiling. Faith Muthoni is, Juan Moreno says, 'a strong woman' who makes 'the best of it'. Taliercio also takes a picture of the standard dish in Muthoni's restaurant. The German visitors include this recipe – along with the one for Madrilenian bull's tail – in their book about cooks and their stories. In Moreno's version, however, it calls for a kilo of white cabbage: this is a vegetable Faith Muthoni uses only on rare occasions, if she happens to find it on the rubbish dump.[41]

*

Marilyn Hagerty is in her mid-eighties. She lives in Grand Forks, North Dakota, a city with a little more than 50,000 inhabitants, halfway between Fargo and the Canadian border. A journalist by profession, she has written for the *Herald*, Grand Forks' local paper, since 1951. Since 1987, she has been reviewing the city's restaurants in the column *Eatbeat*. Polemics aren't Hagerty's thing. Life is different from in the big cities here in Grand Forks, she says. She refuses to attack 'hard-working restaurant people'. If the restaurants are really bad, she won't review them in the first place.

In January 2012, Hagerty visits the Southgate Casino Bar and Grill in Grand Forks. She eats a club sandwich and French fries. She praises the fries: their golden hue, their modest salt content. She praises the sandwich, but finds the cheese a little tasteless and superfluous. She praises the waitress, Rachel, who served the large table efficiently. She has Rachel bag up half of her portion and puts it in the fridge at home. The reader is told all of this, on 11 January 2012. A few days later, Hagerty pays the Blue Moose in East Grand Forks a visit. She finds the menu entertaining, albeit a little confusing. She notes the ribs with Norwegian barbecue sauce. She doesn't order these, however, but instead tries the chicken fajita soup for four dollars. It is very hot, the critic observes, and very substantial. And it is served with exactly the right quantity of crackers.

On 18 January, she shares these thoughts with the public of eastern North Dakota in her column.

A few weeks later, Marilyn Hagerty turns her attentions to the newly opened Olive Garden in Grand Forks, visiting the branch of one of the largest restaurant chains in the United States for a late lunch. She is impressed by the interior design. Following the recommendation of her waitress, she selects the Chicken Alfredo. She doesn't order the equally highly praised raspberry lemonade, but instead sticks with water. It seems very fitting to Hagerty that the salad here, in Olive Garden, includes black olives. She praises the Chicken Alfredo, saying that the serving is generous. In conclusion, she declares the branch of Olive Garden to be the 'biggest and most beautiful restaurant in Grand Forks'. On 7 March 2012, her review is published in the *Herald*. Little does she know that it is about to change her life.[42]

*

The head chef slings his shotgun across his torso. He has taken off his white chef's uniform and pulled on skiwear. He straps on his skis, then makes his way over to the dog enclosure and fetches Krut, his English setter, from his cage. Perhaps he might manage to shoot a bird in the woods today. He skis along the old road to Huså. It was once a boom town, more than a century ago, until all the ore was mined and nature reclaimed the road. Now it is nothing more than a path through the forest. Krut the dog runs through the snow, looping this way and that. The head chef hears an owl. Besides that, there is only silence. He holds his breath, taking it all in.

He shoots nothing today. Back near the restaurant, he cuts a few twigs of juniper and stashes them into his rucksack. Then he stops at the doghouse with Krut, puts him back in the cage, and skis back to the main house. He changes back into chef's whites, sits down at the computer in the kitchen and checks his emails. There are about 150 this morning.

It is the second decade of the twenty-first century, and Magnus Nilsson is the chef of Fäviken in the Swedish province of Jämtlands Iän. Even though he had no hunting success today, there will still be something to eat this evening in the restaurant. Cheese which is just five or six minutes old. Or small vessels made from dried pig's blood, filled with trout roe. Or pork broth, filtered through moss. A few weeks previously, he offered his autumn foliage broth: made with wild mushrooms, a handful of moss, a mixture of this year's foliage (acorn, birch or poplar) and last year's foliage – earthy-smelling brown leaves which are barely distinguishable from the soil. Today there could be a cut of meat from an old dairy cow, dry-aged for seven months, roasted and served on lichens with fermented gooseberries. And once more, because it's what the customers want, he is going to reach for his saw.[43]

*

Over the course of just a few hours, Marilyn Hagerty's report from Olive Garden's newest branch spreads across the entire United States. A blog in Denver publishes the link and further websites follow its lead. Internet foodies from all the big cities point out the unintended comedy of the article. For them, Olive Garden is on a level with chains like Burger King and McDonald's. The fact that, in a city called Grand Forks of all places, there is such an unusually irony-free response to a new standardized catering facility of system gastronomy: well, this seems worthy of attention.

On 8 March 2012, just a day after the publication of her text, Hagerty receives a call from New York City. Camille

Dodero, writer for the *Village Voice*, interviews the journalist and asks for her reaction to the reactions. The response is unsurprising. Hagerty is pleased about the positive feedback and less than pleased about the negative. But the storm doesn't stop with telephone interviews. Anderson Cooper, the star CNN reporter, takes up the story. Hagerty is flown to New York and appears on national breakfast television.[44]

As she's in town anyway, Hagerty is taken out to Le Bernardin – one of the best restaurants in New York. Head chef Eric Ripert gives her a tour of the kitchen. Then he serves her the tasting menu. On the table before Hagerty appear caviar and squid (a first for her), monkfish, an orange sorbet with olive oil and basil, a chocolate ganache with hazelnut mousse and salted caramel ice cream. She likes the cooks' white uniforms, the eloquence of the sommelier and the neat portion sizes. She praises in particular the fact that Le Bernardin has little tables at the ready on which ladies can rest their handbags. Marilyn Hagerty is unable to see many minus points. That's how she writes it up for the *Herald*, her paper back home in Grand Forks, the third largest city in North Dakota.[45]

*

Magnus Nilsson spent three years cooking in the Parisian three-star restaurant L'Astrance: 4 Rue Beethoven, in the 16th arrondissement, on the banks of the Seine, between the Metro stations Passy and Trocadéro. He lived in a tiny room, because a Parisian chef, even at a gourmet restaurant, can't afford anything more there. This was one of the reasons why he left L'Astrance.

Now he is standing in Fäviken, 600 km north of Stockholm, 187 km east of Trondheim, with the saw in his hand. They have much more space here, he and his family. They keep sheep. He slaughters them himself. Though with Valdemar it was difficult and emotional, because he was so charismatic and handsome – Magnus Nilsson gave him one final scratch behind the ear before first pressing the gun to his head and then cutting his throat with the two-bladed knife. In the mornings, driving to the restaurant, after taking his children to kindergarten, he has to watch out for elk crossing the road. His customers fly in to the airport near Ostersund and then take a taxi for the remaining 80 km. They spend the night. Today, the restaurant is fully booked. Fourteen people have gathered here, in a house which to many of them seems as though it's located in the absolute wilderness. They come from all over the world. In the second decade of the twenty-first century, Fäviken is known as one of the best restaurants on the planet. The once influential Michelin rating system and *Gault & Millau* no longer interest globally active gourmets. The list of the world's 50 Best Restaurants now determines the allure of an establishment. Fäviken entered the rankings in 2012, and has remained in the top 50 ever since.[46]

In addition, there is also a manifesto of new Nordic cuisine, signed by René Redzepi, the chef at Noma (number one on the world's 50 Best Restaurants list in 2012) and by colleagues from Finland, Greenland, Norway and the Faroe Islands. Summarized in ten points, the text calls for ecological, conscious cooking which reflects the seasons as well as the 'cleanliness, freshness, simplicity and ethics' which the authors associate with the North.[47] Nilsson's name is not amongst the signatures. But he seems to want to radicalize the philosophy sketched out in the manifesto once again.[48] He serves regional cooking, even though the region where he lives produces no fresh ingredients for six months of the year. He ferments, he dries. He presents the food in a disordered, earthy way. It is intended to be primitive cooking or, in the words of Nilsson's grandfather, 'rektún mat', real food.[49]

Magnus Nilsson's own version of a manifesto is published in 2012 by a London publishing house. In pictures, essays and recipes, *Fäviken* the book tells the story of Fäviken the restaurant. And it reveals this: Magnus Nilsson doesn't actually want to do any more sawing. The dish which requires him to saw is boring him. But he can't change things simply because they bore him. New Nordic cooking is about sincerity, authenticity and nurturing tradition. He can't just stop sawing after a few years.

And so he walks into the dining room with the saw in his hand. The guests' heads turn towards him as he positions himself in front of the old wooden block. He feels their gazes on him. He has to do it.[50]

*

President Xi Jinping goes out to eat. It is a Saturday afternoon in December 2013, and he suddenly appears in the restaurant Qingfeng in western Beijing. No one has announced his visit. When other top Chinese politicians appear in public, they are surrounded by a many-headed entourage. Xi Jinping is accompanied by just two colleagues. Qingfeng is packed, as it always is at lunchtime. The leader of China picks up a tray, orders, pays (twenty-one yuan, around two and a half euros). Wu Songjin is sitting at the cash desk and is shocked, she later tells the press, to see the president here. He sits down at a table with his two companions and eats. Customers and restaurant staff flock round him. Photos are taken. A child goes up to his table. Xi Jinping puts down his chopsticks for a moment and smiles for a smartphone. He eats everything on his plate. And disappears.

From this moment on, nothing in Qingfeng is like it used to be. The restaurant becomes a tourist magnet. Xi's table is renamed the Imperial Seat, and the restaurant management will offer a President Menu with the dishes he selected. They will organize a separate queue for customers who, instead of eating, just want to take photographs. A song is composed about the high-profile visit to the fast-food restaurant, with lyrics such as: 'He stood with us in the queue/paid for his food/carried his plate with his own two hands'. The Chinese censorship authority will instruct the media to tone down the heat of the story and delete online reports about the storm of tourists visiting the restaurant.[51] But this lunch requires further interpretation.

*

Saru Jayaraman, US trade union official and lawyer, is the daughter of Indian immigrants. She grew up surrounded by xenophobia and racism. Youths would shout at her and her family that they should go 'back to Iraq'. And in India relatives commented that she was her parents' darkest child and warned her not to spend too much time in the sun.

But nothing could have prepared her for what she encounters in American restaurants. She feels as though she has been transported to a completely different world. In the more refined city restaurants, the relatively well-paid waiters and waitresses, as well as the bartenders, are white. The badly paid table cleaners and kitchen helpers are not. Almost always, the invisible workers at the back of the restaurant are darker than those at the front. And the racism is masked by vague definitions. The most important thing about service personnel is 'the look', say the owners. And the ability to engage in 'table talk'. They only credit their white employees with this look and conversational competence, and the material disparity which this prejudice produces is immense. In one top New York establishment, the waiters and waitresses, white and often of European descent, earn around $150,000 a year in 2005. The *bussers* – their crockery-clearing helpers – receive a fifth of this sum. Most of them are Latinos.

For Jayaraman, this is the blind spot of new American gourmet culture. The Restaurants Opportunity Center, which she leads, is attending to an industry which operates according to racist codes. Officially speaking, these codes haven't existed in the USA for decades. But in the supposedly multi-cultural culinary world, of all places, they are being kept alive. And the current hyper-attentiveness to ecological and regional concerns seems to stand in the way of decent work conditions and equality, rather than promote them. When Saru Jayaraman goes out to eat with friends, they ask whether the rocket is organic, whether the raspberries are local and the meat in the burgers is from grass-fed cattle. Jayaraman, in contrast, enquires about the ethnic diversity of the waiters and the restaurant's advancement and training policies. And on her way to the toilet, she always has a quick glance into the kitchen.[52]

*

President Xi Jinping's lunch has to be interpreted. Theories are circulating on Weibo, China's version of Twitter. Even the name of the restaurant selected by the great leader must have a deeper meaning. Qingfeng means 'celebrate the harvest', but it also sounds like the words 'clear wind'. Did the President want to call for a war on corruption? Are the winds of change about to blow against corruptible bureaucrats? Xi Jinping ordered spring onions, glazed and sautéed. Is this a call for transparency? He ate roasted pig's liver. Does this mean that government officials, who are greedy like pigs, will be roasted, or in other words fired? Hope in China exists once more, concludes one Weibo user. Just a few weeks after the presidential lunch, a small group of protesters gather in front of Qingfeng restaurant to call for more honesty and humility from politicians. Police quickly break up the demonstration.[53]

*

The hot thighbone of a pig lies before him. Aromas rise up through the air, from the meat, from the fat. And Magnus Nilsson saws. Just a few seconds, then the bone is split in two. He takes one of the two halves, reaches for a long spoon and scoops the marrow out into a pre-warmed bowl. He inspects the mixture to make sure there are no bone splinters in it, no veins or cartilage. Then he mixes it with small pieces of pig's heart and, finally, folds in slivers of turnip. Each guest receives a portion. His colleague Johann explains the dish to them. And Magnus Nilsson disappears back into the kitchen with his saw.

He turns his attention to the next course. He steams dried rosehips in a little butter. Then he deglazes them with raspberry vinegar, before chopping the rosehips finely. He steams fourteen external Brussels sprout leaves. He places small heaps of onions cooked in yoghurt on the plate. Then he takes the sprout leaves and covers each pile of onions with a leaf. Upon that he lays the glazed, finely chopped rosehips. He seasons it with a little salt. Next to the onion–Brussels sprout–rosehip construction he places a small piece of pork. Then fourteen plates are ready to serve. The desserts follow. He doesn't have to do any more sawing for the customers today. After cleaning up, he will look into the notebook where he jots down his observations. He and his colleagues will discuss what went well today and what must be improved. Then he will drive home through the night.[54]

4

READING RESTAURANTS

In 1973, sociologist Daniel Bell published *The Coming of Post-Industrial Society* – it was the same year that Henri Gault and Christian Millau composed the ten commandments of nouvelle cuisine. Bell's predictions were comprehensive. Very soon, his study prophesied, the industrial sector would disappear from view. In its place a post-industrial society would arise, in which theoretical knowledge – instead of production – would be of central importance. This society would be defined by a technical intelligentsia, primarily concerned with disseminating ideas throughout the world, and would no longer be involved in the production of goods.[1]

Neither the restaurant nor nouvelle cuisine plays a role in Bell's visions of an information society.[2] He envisages the university as the pivotal institution of the post-industrial age.[3] But the act of eating out has knowledge-expanding functions. One dines in order to take in ideas and information: about other cultures, new trends, new forms of creativity. Though originating in late eighteenth-century Paris, it was only in late industrial and post-industrial times that the restaurant spread worldwide and on a mass scale. In societies with prosperous middle classes, it has now become an everyday destination.

Many of us live in the future envisioned by this great American sociologist. Intellectual and creative work has supplanted physically demanding activities.[4] We look at the meagre portions on the plates before us and find ourselves in Daniel Bell's world. Shaped by knowledge circulation and manifestos of nouvelle cuisine, the post-industrial society doesn't prioritize the speedy intake of calories. No longer obliged to perform manual activities, middle- and upper-class bodies have taken on more aesthetic functions. We produce symbols and consume symbols.[5] Seeking sophistication rather than satiation, customers in high-class restaurants demonstrate this shift in eating habits, for themselves and for others.[6] And the early twenty-first-century 'techno-emotional cuisine' of Ferran Adrià or Heston Blumenthal, with its wealth of references, its complexity, its science, seems like something Bell dreamed up to illustrate his theories. The elite restaurant, where waiters introduce each course of a tasting menu with a lengthy explanation of its complex nuances, has become a laboratory of the information society.

*

This is how we could read restaurants today. But the perspective would be too narrow. Because far more present than the experiments of a few genius chefs are the fast-food chains of our time. George Ritzer's interpretations of the way we eat and work seem much closer to our reality than Daniel Bell's. In his studies of 'McDonaldization', Ritzer shows us a world shaped by the service industry, in which work itself is just as standardized as consumption.[7] Human feelings are commercialized and controlled through the proliferation and disciplining of service.[8] Fast-food chains don't just produce metaphors of efficiency and uniformity. They transform the world around them as well, simply because they're everywhere.

Numerous observations support Ritzer's theories of the service society. In the 1990s, for example, more people were employed in the Indian restaurants of Great Britain than in the British shipbuilding and steel industries combined.[9] For one thing, gastronomy has developed into a central branch of the economy. For another, waiter-like behaviour is expected ever more frequently outside of restaurants. Regardless of the occupation, work is now rewarded with gratuityesque, performance-based salary bonuses or, in turn, punished by their withdrawal.

In this sense, waitresses and waiters from the late nineteenth and early twentieth centuries were messengers from the future. To the disconcertment of observers at the time (like Sartre and Orwell) they earned their money not with measurable physical effort, but with emotional work. They smiled, made small talk, conveyed positive feelings to their customers. They were representatives of themselves, and often, in addition, representatives of their own ethnic identities. For that they received tip money, in remuneration rituals which seemed irrational at first glance, and very strange within the industrial context. Today, however, these work and payment structures are part of everyday life.[10] Today, we are all waiters.

Furthermore, service jobs in the food sector symbolize and accelerate the development towards unstable, non-unionized, underpaid workplaces. For the working poor, McJobs are often the only option – and these jobs devalue work as such.[11] In the United States, progress has been made in recent years with unionizing fast-food employees. But the surprised reaction when McDonald's staff go on strike demonstrates how little respect service workers can count on.[12] McJobs show, in plain view, how working conditions in post-industrial capitalism have become increasingly unstable and unprotected.[13] The service proletariat behind the counters reveal Bell's vision of a polity of highly educated technocrats to be an extremely optimistic fiction.[14]

*

Somewhere between Bell's dream of the information society and Ritzer's nightmare of a McDonaldized world, the restaurant serves up reality. It is both: a place that generates new forms of creative innovation, and a site of exploitative labour. Most importantly, restaurants are driven by artisanal and quasi-industrial work. If anyone should think that in the Western metropolis, physical exertion and manual labour disappeared along with the last factories, they only need to look at the 20,000 plus restaurants of New York City, the 30,000 restaurants of Paris, the 160,000 restaurants of Tokyo. These businesses rely on the hard physical toil of their personnel: day after day and late into the night.[15] Chefs and kitchen staff work with their hands – with ingredients and simple tools. At the dining tables, members of the new, supposedly disembodied era may chat away. But back in the kitchen, people are sweating, carrying heavy loads, dicing up food, washing plates and pots and pans. This work leaves its mark on their bodies, with pain, burns and scars.[16]

Communication, too, so important for the post-industrial information society, functions differently in the kitchen. Beyond the TV food programmes, professional chefs do not see themselves as masters of language. Sociologist Gary Alan Fine has shown how many chefs cannot or will not verbally justify why a dish has succeeded or failed.[17] It's not that their actions and practices are primitive. They are just rarely wordy. The knowledge chefs acquire is formed not so much by the theory circuits of the information age, but by extensive bodily practice. Handling a knife professionally, for example, demands precise coordination.[18] The restaurant, therefore, is a terrain of physicality – and a highly interesting one. Philosopher Matthew Crawford, for instance, watches a short-order cook working under pressure and observes in his handling of the ingredients, knives, heat and pans something which cognitive scientists are constantly discussing these days: that humans don't just think with their brains, but also with their bodies.[19] For waitresses and waiters – who combine their athletic condition with an almost dancer-like dexterity[20] – similar conclusions can be drawn.

*

Behind the kitchen door, there are breadline wages, incidents of physical violence, and immigrants without papers who are mercilessly exposed to the whims of their employers.[21] This has piqued the curiosity of generations of observers. George Orwell and Saru Jayaraman argue in each of their respective periods that gastronomic work must be investigated and its conditions reformed. The restaurant reminds consumers that the physical labour they may consider anachronistic doesn't just continue to exist in kitchens, but also in other sectors of the economy; such as those which depend upon the output of Cambodian textile factories or Congolese mines. Unlike fashion boutiques and electronics stores, however, the restaurant makes the simultaneity of pleasure and hard work evident for every consumer. Real people, just a few metres away in the kitchen, attest to the social inequality produced by consumer capitalism.[22] And never have chefs been such explicitly public figures as they are today. The kitchen is no longer a closed-off craft space. Television formats, magazines, coffee-table books and documentary films provide detailed insights. Numerous restaurants renowned for their innovative style have long since introduced the open kitchen, allowing customers to watch the chefs as they work.

The open kitchens of trend-setting restaurants are often served by *prep kitchens*: hidden, inaccessible basement spaces as large as the restaurant itself.[23] This is a telling example that the curious gaze on cooking has much more to do with 'eating right' than with a genuine interest in social justice. 'Good food' provides today's middle classes with purpose.[24] Whether in the restaurant, at home or on the screen, it satisfies various desires. According to Adam Gopnik, food may serve as a new religion or as a kind of sport, a status symbol, a substitute for sex, or as a moral ritual.[25] And this sounds plausible. Seeing previously closed-off restaurant kitchens on TV stills our hunger for intense, authentic images. In a time when fewer of us are cooking for ourselves, we are becoming increasingly interested in media representations of food preparation.[26] As consumers of the digital, we long for the analogue and supposedly primitive – and this we associate with the manual labour carried out in the kitchen, with the sometimes gentle, sometimes violent preparation of food. The more authentic the restaurant, the higher its value. This applies particularly to postmodern cities, where authenticity is often an important part of the sales pitch for estate agents and gastronomes alike.[27]

This growing interest in restaurant work is fuelled by authors doing double duty as consumers and public intellectuals. The restaurant critics of the late twentieth century, as specialized as they were hedonistic, have been replaced by food writers whose skills seem to extend far beyond the evaluation of five-course menus. These gastro-thinkers have established transparency as a key value when it comes to food. They tell consumers that they should, nay must, know more about where their food comes from. That it is their moral and political duty to observe the production processes behind their food.[28] Slow-food activist Carlo Petrini, for example, calls upon diners to discover their nourishment's place of origin, to study the 'history of a dish', and to imagine the 'hands of those' who were involved in its production. For Petrini, knowledge and pleasure are inextricably linked.[29] Whether opened up by architecture, visual media or food writing, the kitchen now features a control window. Knowledge-hungry consumers gaze through it – encouraged by the culinary intellectuals of our time.

We could celebrate this as the dawn of a new, more critical food culture.[30] For a long time, gourmet gastronomy was defined by French expertise and therefore less by individual expression than by the organized system of haute cuisine. As that influence has declined, and new gastronomic scenes have blossomed, restaurants have now become stages for non-conformist, even activist cooking. In California, Copenhagen, Sydney or Berlin, a restaurant's quality is no longer measured by loyalty to a Parisian ideal, but instead by its own wealth of ideas, its originality.[31] Gastronomy is also taking on a political role at the interface between food practices and globalized capitalism: in the battle against monocultures or in struggles against the exploitation of resources and people by food manufacturers.[32]

Seen from this angle, we could describe Chez Panisse, a restaurant shaped by the philosophy of sustainability, as a critique of a 'technocratic dictatorship'.[33] Ecologically aware cooks are questioning the industrialization of foodstuffs. They are developing forms of regional cooking, constructing local networks, particularly in collaboration with small-scale farmers. Anthropologist Amy Trubek extols this restaurant model as 'grassroots postmodernism'.[34] Some celebrated gastronomes are no longer perceived as business people, but as enlightened mediators between trade and ethics.[35]

All this, however, doesn't mean that the pressure on restaurants will slacken. Contemporary foodies may not apply the rigorous standards of haute cuisine.[36] They may seek culinary fulfilment both in restaurants and at food trucks. And they may be progressive and unelitist. But they still make demands. Instead of looking for refinement and elegance, foodies eating out want to find credible signs of authenticity and sustainability. So the staging may be new, but it still has to be right. If a long-haired chef in northern Sweden has become known around the planet for sawing bones, then he must continue to saw bones. Furthermore, and unlike the gourmets of old, twenty-first-century foodies have at their disposal a variety of media platforms for evaluating and critiquing gastronomic failures and achievements: blogs, social networks, review sites.[37] Restaurants thus operate in a late-modern era in which the 'creativity ideal', as Andreas Reckwitz observes, has forced its way into 'dominant segments of contemporary culture' and 'changed into an obligatory societal regime'.[38] Gastronomy, too, bows to this imperative. In the restaurant – sometimes beloved, sometimes denounced – it becomes evident how the combined forces of commercialism and fashion place human protagonists under pressure. This happens not in spite of, but precisely because the foodie expects personal expression, sustainability and creative authenticity on the plate.

*

Toiling and sweating cooks and waiters should not distract us, then, from the fact that the culinary is endlessly verbalized and theorized. Although the majority of kitchen staff work in anonymity, various members of the profession seem obliged to transform themselves into media personalities. Appearing on cookery shows, writing recipe books and autobiographies, philosophizing about food: this is all now part of certain chefs' job descriptions.[39] Take Jacques Pépin, for example, who in postwar France was a member of a craft guild which stamped out any signature flourish, any hint of individuality from kitchen staff. In the late twentieth-century United States, Pépin became a highly visible individual: a television cook, an author, a business adviser and university professor.[40] From the 'fusion food' wave to Nordic cuisine, an ever-growing number of innovative culinary 'schools' are emerging.[41] Simpler cuisines attest to this development too – and this doesn't only apply to the legendary Chez Panisse and its highly educated kitchen staff.[42] A contemporary textbook declares the 'iconic chef', the 'visionary chef' and the 'innovator chef' to be the three highest levels of a cook's identity.[43]

By contrast, globalized fast-food enterprises focus on differentiated planning, convenience food and controlled innovation processes. The emphasis is certainly not on personal expression, but on the precise production of desires and, subsequently, their industrial fulfilment. Scientific studies play a key role in this. The success of McDonald's, for example, can be interpreted as a perfect example of Taylorist principles, and by the same token so can the company's most recent failures, attributable to their inaccurate investigations into customer tastes (which now tend more towards freshness and health rather than speed and comfort).[44] The independent restaurant, built upon individual creativity, seems like the utopian antithesis to the chains and their systems.

But even the quirkiest, most visionary top chefs of non-chain restaurants work in teams they lead and organize systematically. The mastering of complex logistics is just as important to their working day as the careful planning of work processes. A major American study has shown that any restaurant's success or failure is not due primarily to the quality or popularity of its dishes, but rather to its 'operating philosophy' and how well-defined its concept is.[45] According to one culinary expert, the most advanced chefs of our time are 'comparable to the leaders of large scientific and medicinal institutes'.[46] Even as the supposed sensory antithesis to Taylorist chain gastronomy, the non-chain restaurant still shows clear traits of scientification – emerging slowly in the nineteenth and early twentieth centuries, gaining pace throughout the twentieth century, and exploding in our present day, where it now seems perfectly normal for restaurant critics to compose manifestos on 'culinary intelligence'.[47]

*

Like the cinema, the department store and the beach, the restaurant is an openly accessible place. We could read it as a typical landscape of the 'open society' envisioned by philosopher Karl Popper. Amongst strangers, acquaintances and friends, 'personal relationships of a new kind' can come into being here: connections not determined by 'accidents of birth'.[48] The restaurant is not a meeting place for the 'tribal community' (something Popper, a Jewish refugee, abhorred). The customer has gone to a public space and now opens up his body to food which a stranger has prepared for him.[49] Anyone who visits the restaurant is taking a step, as a member of Popper's open society, into 'the unknown, into the uncertain and insecure'.[50]

For travellers in the Middle Ages and early modern period, being catered for was an unavoidable necessity.[51] In the twentieth and twenty-first centuries, however, the restaurant visit becomes mostly voluntary. To eat together, to drink, to entrust oneself to others' care: this turns the restaurant into a place where the open society is both celebrated and lived out every day. A huge variety of gastronomic options have developed for the growing middle classes: for those in a hurry, for romantics, for those interested in ethnic cuisine, for those who want local food, for those with refined tastes and those leaning more toward the rustic.[52] But as specific as a restaurant's self-identification may be: it functions as an accessible part of the social fabric.

It is telling that some early twenty-first-century multi-millionaires no longer seek out restaurants, but instead hire gourmet chefs to 'curate' culinary events.[53] In contrast to such practices, a visit to even the most elite of establishments seems like an affirmation of public space and sociability. A humble local reporter like Marilyn Hagerty, swept from North Dakota to Manhattan by the serendipity of internet hype, can investigate the merits of the luxurious Le Bernardin and tell her readers all about it. Even the gourmet restaurant is open when it's open. And it is the very opposite to this openness that makes racist codes in restaurant history so apparent. When Gerta Pfeffer and David Grünspecht are cursed at in Nazi Germany's inns, Popper's juxtaposition of tribal community and open society becomes particularly clear and frightening.

*

Alexandros Stefanidis grew up in his parents' Greek restaurant in Karlsruhe, Germany. Now a successful journalist, he reports that he still has dreams in which he sees himself bringing 'plates of gyros' to tables. Stefanidis looks back to his childhood and sees his family's 'ethnic' restaurant as a kind of living room: never 'a closed society', but instead the 'dream of an open one', in a country his parents had arrived in as 'guest workers', but soon became hosts.[54]

Stefanidis's account is one of countless stories of 'ethnic encounters' in restaurants: between minorities and mainstream society, between and amongst different minorities. Tastes, decorations, languages or fragments of speech and differing cultural styles lead to the creation of cosmopolitan zones in culinary establishments.[55] International gastronomy may have the power to turn cultures hostile towards immigration into more open societies.[56]

Nonetheless, even the most enthusiastic imbibing of exotic delicacies does not necessarily demonstrate intercultural understanding. Stanley Fish gets to the heart of this. He describes 'boutique multiculturalism' as an attitude which, despite happily seeking pleasure in the restaurants of the 'other', is not prepared to have its own cultural and moral values called into question. Interesting sensual details may liven up the everyday life of individuals and their consumer choices. But when it comes down to it, the 'boutique multi-culturalist' may be nothing more than a closet xenophobe who likes varied dining options.[57] And from an urbanist perspective, restaurants, however ethnically diverse their menus may claim to be, can play key roles in the gentrification of urban neighbourhoods, and thereby intensify the homogenization of contemporary cities rather than their plurality.[58]

Then again, cultural exchange certainly takes place on the palate as well. New culinary practices allow cultural differences to circulate, opening up societies on a sensory level too. In early twentieth-century London, the internationality of the Empire led to a diversification of culinary choices. In the twenty-first century, the hunger for the 'exotic' is so much a part of everyday life that it has long since become an advertising cliché. And the transformation doesn't just play out in restaurants explicitly coded as 'ethnic'. El Bulli can only be understood as a hybrid phenomenon: as a mix of German-Czech longing for the Mediterranean, French nouvelle cuisine, the rediscovery of Catalan everyday culture and the now-worldwide curiosity of gourmets and cooks. The exploration of such transcultural relationships seems more productive if we give less credence to problematic notions of originality. Critics emphasize how vacuous the concepts of 'authentic' ethnic cooking are – though marketing campaigns take them up eagerly. Anyone turning their attention to chefs in the hybrid zones between nations and cultures today should go not in search of 'authenticity', but the messy intercultural practices themselves.[59]

Whether the restaurant really helps to engender a heterogeneous society open to all kinds of authentic influences is therefore something which optimists and pessimists will view very differently. So-called 'ethnic cuisine' has surely produced as many clichés and misunderstandings as it has enlightening interactions. The chicken tikka masala may have been declared the new British national dish at the beginning of the twenty-first century – but the widespread practice of the takeaway could also indicate that many customers prefer to surrender themselves to exoticism only for very short periods of time.[60] In the United States, the restaurant shows itself to be a terrain where blatant laws of exclusion were closely followed by unwritten codes which are no less discriminatory.[61] In recent German history, easily accessible Turkish fast-food stands became sites and symbols of deadly hate crimes.[62] Discussing Western–Eastern culinary interactions, Robert Ji-Song Ku coined the expression 'dubious gastronomy'. He exposes how Western clientele insert Chinese food, MSG or 'inauthentic sushi' into an orientalist discourse about suspect minorities.[63]

Sociologist Krishnendu Ray calls upon scholars to go beyond the exploration of consumption in ethnic restaurants. He himself concentrates on production and selling. Ray creates nuanced portraits of men and women running Pakistani grill restaurants in New York City. He sees these hard-working men and women as designers: of the food, of the restaurants they manage, of the mediation they provide between South Asian and American culture. Immigration engenders and transports knowledge. In the simple Pakistani restaurants where Krishnendu Ray conducts his research, this knowledge can be explored in spaces, practices, tastes and smells.[64] Nonetheless, it would be naive to assume that immigrants in gastronomic establishments are allowed to consistently 'live' their culture. Melinda Nadj Abonji's *Fly Away, Pigeon* depicts this particularly eloquently. Self-discipline and masking are basic elements of survival in the trade.

*

Are Woolworth's lunch counters really restaurants? Are kebab stands? And the burger franchises where Robin Leidner learned the correct way to smile? Gourmets will disagree. Rebecca Spang, for example, defines restaurants as establishments which enable individualized and personalized service.[65] Alfred Kölling's classic German *Textbook for Waiters* defines the restaurant as a public space which 'offers varied dishes and sophisticated drinks in well-furnished rooms'.[66] These categorizations seem reasonable – and much narrower than the one used here.

In our complicated reality, however, defining a restaurant seems much more difficult. Burger branches may not be particularly renowned for their 'well-furnished rooms', yet the McDonald's group never tires of calling them 'restaurants'. Numerous snack bars, with rather limited choices, display the moniker 'restaurant' above their entrances. And colloquially we speak of 'going to a restaurant' whether we are paying several hundred euros for a Michelin-star dinner or just ten euros for a pizza and a Coke. Much like the definition of 'art', that of 'restaurant' is a valorizing term. Winston Churchill was aware of this when he christened wartime feeding stations as 'British Restaurants'. The 'Lobby Restaurant' in Cologne could serve as a telling example; founded in 1994 as a restaurant for the homeless, it aims to provide not just food but also forms of sociability otherwise lacking in its guests' lives.[67] What a restaurant is and is not, therefore, even gourmets cannot conclusively define. The practice shapes the definition.

It is helpful at this point to remember Howard Becker's sociology of art, which consciously embraces the marginal phenomena of a system in order to discover more about the mechanisms and decision processes at its core.[68] This book operates with a broad definition of the restaurant: as a public space where people can eat when they want, what they want and as much as they want for a previously established price.[69] This reflects the dynamic of gastronomy, an extremely flexible industry adapting itself constantly to shifting cultural trends and new forms of appetite.[70] The simplest snack establishments are never far removed from gourmet restaurants, because traces of everyday cuisine and simplicity are always present even in the most refined culinary art.[71] In today's foodie culture, the border between cafeteria and restaurant is barely distinguishable anyhow. And so this book's definition of the restaurant remains open, perhaps provocatively so.

*

Restaurant critic Jürgen Dollase regards certain food-studies scholars as 'freeloaders' who presume they can 'succeed in this sector without much effort'.[72] The reprimand is clear. But it seems to fall on deaf ears. Culinary studies has established itself as a vibrant field of research. It sees food, with reference to Marcel Mauss, as a 'total social phenomenon'. It approaches the production and consumption of foodstuffs as 'multidimensional and multidisciplinary cultural studies', or, with a nod to Epikur and Rousseau – 'gastrosophy'.[73]

In this abundantly flourishing discourse, the restaurant has been interpreted frequently, too frequently, from the perspective of the customer. Joanne Finkelstein's works, for example, address *en détail* the codifications at the table.[74] Pierre Bourdieu's analyses serve as models here: the antithesis between 'quantity and quality', and 'the most filling and most economical foods', for example, and what the contrast between 'substance' and 'form' betrays about tastes and class identities.[75] The restaurant makes mechanisms of distinction visible; of this, scholars remind us again and again.[76]

It is time, however, to look at not only the subtle differences in the gastronomic world but also the more obvious ones.[77] A discussion entirely focused on how to distinguish between middle-class and upper-middle-class dining choices runs the risk of overlooking a great deal: the inequality between illegal kitchen workers and globally celebrated chefs, the contrasts between the gossiping customers of luxury restaurants and civil rights activists dragged from a lunch counter, between the service workers on the poverty line and food writers offering their services to either tear apart or praise gourmet refinement.

In view of these contrasts, the nuanced semiotics of culinary phenomena seems less pressing than an exploration of the different backgrounds, needs and approaches of the various people involved with restaurants – as chefs, waiters, critics or customers. Anthropologists David Beriss and David Sutton define the restaurant as an 'ideal postmodern institution'. To them, this is where everything that interests students of culture comes together: production, consumption, exchange, the sensory, the symbolic, the local and global.[78] French sociologist Jean-Pierre Hassoun emphasizes how rare it is to have one place where both intimate pleasures and social ambitions can be explored.[79] In the restaurant as a narrowly limited space, people collide with people and ideas with ideas. In this book these collisions are made tangible.

*

The story told here owes a great deal to the flexible gastronomic job market. The restaurant offers intellectuals a temporary home – as diners, for one thing, and when they want to leave their role as customers behind and immerse themselves in the unknown world beyond the kitchen door or on the other side of service interactions. Anyone who sets their mind to becoming a waiter will, as a rule, find a job. For a kitchen worker too, and even a cook, access to the restaurant is relatively easy, depending on the status and desirability of the establishment in question. Many waitresses, waiters and kitchen workers move on to other sectors of society. But their memories remain.

It is this form of openness that makes the restaurant such an important object for cultural and social reflection. In its approximately 250-year history, it has inspired much more than just food criticism and cookbooks: biographies, autobiographies, reportage, pamphlets, notes, manifestos, novels and academic studies. Observers like Frances Donovan, George Orwell, Bill Buford and Barbara Ehrenreich profited from the fact that it is easy to become someone else from one day to the next, part of a foreign social class, part of that sworn-in community of culinary workers.[80] The restaurant, so open to newcomers, becomes a laboratory in which they can constantly reflect: on consumption, presentation, work, inequality.

And the first three chapters of this book are dedicated to the memories, ideas and stories formed in this lab. Their authors don't have much in common. Some are established scholars; others engage in research on their own initiative. Some spend almost their entire lives in gastronomy; others seem more like *flâneurs*. From their perspectives, a larger picture evolves which is just as contradictory as the restaurant itself.

Simply telling these stories, without interpreting them, can be unproblematic. This book's material refers to individual cases which may not be representative.[81] And their connection to reality is complicated. 'Participatory observation' may inspire exciting research and, consequently, interesting texts. But somewhere in the area of conflict between participation, observation and writing, objectivity evaporates.[82] In addition, some of the authors represented here prompt the unanswered question of whether the fascination with another social class stands in the way of any serious contemplation of social difference.[83]

Nonetheless, the scenes reproduced in the first three chapters of this book are not analysed or deconstructed. Instead the power of the stories and the effect of the montage take centre stage.[84] This approach has aesthetic and pragmatic motivations. The American author David Shields, for example, praises narrative that straddles the divide between fact and fiction. The complex assertion that 'this may be based on real events' doesn't need to be a stigma, Shields notes, but instead can be an inspiring concept.[85] Such ideas are important for this book, because the restaurant, too, is a place divided into public and secret zones, a place which produces legends as well as sustenance and truths. Gastronomic myths and fictions are inextricably linked with more reality-based diagnoses developed by chefs and waitresses, critics and academics. And there is no better technique than the montage for producing that sense of 'being amongst others' which is so unique to the restaurant.

Almost all the documents used here highlight the particular dynamic and intensity of the gastronomic existence. In the restaurant, a hotspot of modernity, experiences reach boiling point. The body works and feels in a particularly profound way. Enthusiasm, disgust, joy, hustle and bustle, the sense of belonging or exclusion are felt more keenly here than elsewhere. In order to bring this intensity to life, some methodological sophistication had to be sacrificed. The material had to be served up almost raw.

NOTES

1. OPENING TIMES

1 Frances Donovan, *The Woman Who Waits* [1920] (New York: Arno, 1974), pp. 17–18; Heather Paul Kurent, 'Frances R. Donovan and the Chicago School of Sociology: A Case Study in Marginality', unpublished dissertation (University of Maryland, 1982), pp. 53, 80–1. Here and subsequently, the locations and situations depicted, along with the actions, impressions and thoughts of historical protagonists, originate not from the author's imagination, but instead from the texts cited in these endnotes (autobiographies, journalistic reports, essays, academic texts, cookbooks and, on occasion, fictional works). Word-for-word quotations are marked as such in the text.

2 Cited in Joanna Waley-Cohen, 'The Quest for Perfect Balance: Taste and Gastronomy in Imperial China', in *Food: The History of Taste*, ed. Paul Freedman (London: Thames & Hudson, 2007), p. 112 (pp. 99–132).

3 Rebecca Spang, 'Restaurants', in *Encyclopedia of Food and Culture*, vol. III, ed. Solomon Katz (New York: Scribner, 2003), p. 180 f. (pp. 179–86).

4 Both Rebecca Spang and Stephen Mennell question the widespread assumption that restaurants began when French cooks formerly employed in the royal courts moved into gastronomy: Rebecca Spang, *The Invention of the Restaurant: Paris and Modern Gastronomic Culture* (Cambridge: Harvard University Press, 2000), p. 67, and Stephen Mennell, *All Manners of Food: Eating and Taste in England and France from the Middle Ages to the Present* (Urbana, IL: University of Illinois Press, 1996), pp. 137–9.

5 Donovan, *The Woman Who Waits*, pp. 7–8, 11, 107.

6 Jürgen Habermas, *The Structural Transformation of the Public Sphere: An Inquiry into a Category of Bourgeois Society* [1962] (Cambridge: MIT Press, 1991), p. 97; Ludger Schwarte, *Philosophie der Architektur* (Munich: Wilhelm Fink, 2009), pp. 230–3.

7 Spang, *Invention*, pp. 86–7.

8 A contemplation of the restaurant (the Vacossins' establishment, around 1777) composed by Rousseau also associates the new gastronomic institution more with intimacy and privacy than public concerns (Spang, *Invention*, p. 59 f.).

9 On gender politics in the American context: Paul Freedman, 'Women and Restaurants in the Nineteenth-Century United States', in *Journal of Social History* 48/1 (2014): 1–19.

10 Plummer points out that the definition the 'Chicago School' was not used for the first time until the 1930s, and that it suggests far greater coherence than is actually evidenced in the heterogeneous methods of the Chicago sociologists (Ken Plummer, 'Introduction', in *The Chicago School: Critical Assessments*, vol. I: *A Chicago Canon?*, ed. Ken Plummer (London: Routledge, 1997), pp. 4–5 (pp. 3–40).

11 Plummer, 'Introduction', p. 8.

12 Park, cited in Plummer, 'Introduction', p. 30.

13 Gert von Paczensky and Anna Dünnebier, *Kulturgeschichte des Essens und Trinkens* (Munich: Orbis, 1999), p. 138.

14 Spang, 'Restaurants', p. 182; Paczensky/Dünnebier, *Kulturgeschichte des Essens und Trinkens*, p. 138.

15 Robert Appelbaum, *Dishing It Out: In Search of the Restaurant Experience* (London: Reaktion, 2011), p. 63. Spang observes that most contemporary readers will not pick up on the satirical moment in Grimod's almanac. Cultural criticism and political satire are just as ignored as the artificiality of the gourmand as a figure. Restaurant criticism emerged as an art form which addresses one thing alone: eating and drinking as a world world unto itself, cut off from everything else (Spang, *Invention*, pp. 158–9).

16 Priscilla Parkhurst Ferguson, *Accounting for Taste: The Triumph of French Cuisine* (Chicago, IL: University of Chicago Press, 2004), p. 11.

17 Ferguson, *Accounting for Taste*, pp. 10–11.

18 Spang, *Invention*, pp. 238–41.

19 Donovan, *The Woman Who Waits*, pp. 20–30.

20 N. N., *Ball's Splendid Mammoth Pictorial Tour of the United States Comprising Views of the African Slave Trade; of Northern and Southern Cities; of Cotton and Sugar Plantations; of the Mississippi, Ohio and Susquehanna Rivers, Niagara Falls, & c: Compiled for the Panorama* (Cincinnati, OH: Achilles Pugh, 1855), p. 41, cited in Deborah Willis (ed.), *J. P. Ball: Daguerrean and Studio Photographer* (New York: Garland, 1993), p. 284 (pp. 243–99).

21 Jean-Robert Pitte, 'The Rise of the Restaurant', in Albert Sonnenfeld (ed.), *Food: A Culinary History from Antiquity to the Present* (New York: Columbia University Press, 2000), p. 475.

22 Spang, 'Restaurants', p. 182.

23 Julius Behlendorff, *Der Oberkellner und Hotel-Secretair: Anleitung zur fachwissenschaftlichen und praktischen Hotel-Führung* [1893]

(Leipzig: Blüher, 1898), pp. 66–7. Here and in subsequent references where only a German-language text is cited, the quotation has been translated into English by the translator of this book.

24 Alessandro Filippini, *The Table: How to Buy Food, How to Cook It, and How to Serve It* (New York: Charles L. Webster, 1889).

25 Andrew F. Smith, *Eating History: 30 Turning Points in the Making of American Cuisine* (New York: Columbia University Press, 2011), p. 22.

26 Joëlle Bonnin-Ponnier, *Le restaurant dans le roman naturaliste: Narration et evaluation* (Paris: Honoré Champion, 2002).

27 Spang, *Invention*, p. 177; Émile Zola, *The Belly of Paris* [1873], translated by Mark Kurlansky (New York: The Modern Library, 2009).

28 Donovan, *The Woman Who Waits*, p. 115.

29 Ibid., p. 171.

30 Ibid., p. 79.

31 Brenda Assael, 'Gastro-Cosmopolitanism and the Restaurant in Late Victorian and Edwardian London', in *The Historical Journal* 56/3 (2013): 681–706.

32 Patrick Rambourg, *Histoire de la cuisine et de la gastronomie françaises: Du Moyen Âge au XXe siècle* (Paris: Perrin, 2010), p. 257.

33 Marie Louise Ritz, cited in Elliott Shore, 'The Development of the Restaurant', in *Food: The History of Taste*, p. 326 (pp. 301–33).

34 Timothy Shaw, *The World of Escoffier* (New York: Vendome, 1995), p. 71.

35 Spang, 'Restaurants', p.182; Shore, 'The Development of the Restaurant', p. 323.

36 Shore, 'The Development of the Restaurant', p. 327.

37 Shaw, *The World of Escoffier*, pp. 119–21.

38 Rambourg, *Histoire de la cuisine et de la gastronomie françaises*, pp. 260–1.

39 Cited in Mennell, *All Manners of Food*, p. 159.

40 Donovan, *The Woman Who Waits*, pp. 106–11.

41 Ibid., p. 145.

42 Ibid., p. 228.

43 Ibid., p. 226.

44 Ibid., p. 224.

45 Ibid., pp. 224–6.

46 Guido Ara, *Der moderne Kellner* (Cologne: Hub. Schleypen, 1909).

47 Marcel Proust, *In Search of Lost Time: In the Shadow of Young Girls in Flower* (New Haven, CT: Yale University Press, 2015), pp. 425–8.

48 Karl-Heinz Glaser, *Aschingers 'Bierquellen' erobern Berlin: Aus dem Weinort Oberderdingen in die aufstrebende Hauptstadt* (Heidelberg: Verlag Regionalkultur, 2004), pp. 65–82, 150; Robert Walser, 'Aschinger' [1907], in Robert Walser, *Sämtliche Werke in Einzelausgaben*, vol. 3: *Aufsätze*, ed. Jochen Greven (Frankfurt: Suhrkamp, 1985), pp. 67–70.

49 Andrew P. Haley, *Turning the Tables: Restaurants and the Rise of the*

American Middle Class, 1880–1920 (Chapel Hill, NC: University of North Carolina Press, 2011), p. 234.

50 Shore, 'The Development of the Restaurant', p. 320; on the automat: Angelika Epple, 'The "Automat": A History of Technological Transfer and the Process of Global Standardization in Modern Fast Food around 1900', in Food and History 7/2 (2009): 97–118.

51 Smith, Eating History, p. 52; for other theories on the origin of the hamburger, see Josh Ozersky, The Hamburger (New Haven, CT: Yale University Press, 2008), pp. 15–17.

52 Inge Huber, Curnonsky oder Das Geheimnis des Maurice-Edmond Sailland (Munich: Collection Rolf Heyne, 2010), pp. 204–6.

53 Haley, Turning the Tables, p. 222.

54 Kurent, Frances R. Donovan and the Chicago School of Sociology, pp. 86–8.

55 Mary Jo Deegan, 'The Chicago Men and the Sociology of Women', in The Chicago School: Critical Assessments, vol. I : A Chicago Canon?, ed. Ken Plummer (London: Routledge, 1997), pp. 198–230.

56 Robert E. Park, 'Introduction', in Frances Donovan, The Saleslady (Chicago, IL: University of Chicago Press, 1929), pp. vii–ix.

57 Frances Donovan, The Schoolma'am (New York: Frederick A. Stokes, 1939).

58 Joseph Roth, 'Die Bar des Volkes' [1920], in Wiebke Porombka (ed.), Trübsal einer Straßenbahn: Stadtfeuilletons von Joseph Roth (Salzburg: Jung und Jung, 2012) pp. 41–4.

59 Wilhelm von Sternburg, Joseph Roth: Eine Biographie (Cologne: Kiepenheuer & Witsch, 2009), p. 543.

60 Sternburg, Joseph Roth, pp. 205–7.

61 Wiebke Porombka, 'Nachwort', in Trübsal, pp. 254–5 (pp. 253–67).

62 Roth, 'Die Bar des Volkes', p. 44.

63 Cited in Gail Levin, Edward Hopper: An Intimate Biography (New York: Rizzoli, 2007), p. 141.

64 Levin, Edward Hopper, p. 201.

65 Coe shows that Chinese restaurants are already a major part of everyday life in America by this point in time: Andrew Coe, Chop Suey: A Cultural History of Chinese Food in the United States (Oxford: Oxford University Press, 2009), p. 198.

66 Ivo Kranzfelder, Edward Hopper (Cologne: Taschen, 2002), p. 155.

67 Walter Wells, Silent Theater: The Art of Edward Hopper (London: Phaidon, 2007), p. 240.

68 Allyson Nadia Field, 'Expatriate Lifestyle as Tourist Destination: The Sun Also Rises and Experiential Travelogues of the Twenties', in Mark Cirino and Mark P. Ott (eds), Ernest Hemingway and the Geography of Memory (Kent, OH: Kent State University Press, 2010), pp. 83–96.

69 George Orwell, Down and Out in Paris and London [1933] (Orlando: Harcourt, 1961), pp. 6–121; Gordon Bowker, George Orwell (London: Little, Brown and Company, 2003), pp. 96–153.

70 Joseph Roth, 'Der Koch in der Küche' [1929], in Joseph Roth, *Panoptikum: Gestalten und Kulissen* (Cologne: Kiepenheuer & Witsch, 1983), pp. 52–6.

71 Achim Küpper, 'Berichte aus der Fremde: Unbehaustheit als Grundmotiv von Joseph Roths Reisereportagen und Reiseschilderungen', Thomas Eicher (ed.), in *Joseph Roth und die Reportage* (Heidelberg: Mattes, 2010), pp. 112–14 (pp. 99–125).

72 Roth, 'Der Koch in der Küche', pp. 52–6.

73 Orwell, *Down and Out*, pp. 105–15.

74 Bowker, *George Orwell*, p. 142.

75 Gerald Hogan, *Selling 'em by the Sack: White Castle and the Creation of American Food* (New York: New York University Press, 1999), p. 27.

76 Ibid., pp. 30–1.

77 Ibid., p. 45.

78 Ibid., p. 33.

79 M. F. K. Fisher, *Long Ago in France: The Years in Dijon* (New York: Touchstone, 1992), pp. 29–34.

80 M. F. K. Fisher, 'Consider the Oyster' [1941], in M. F. K. Fisher, *The Art of Eating* (London: Papermac, 1991), p. 125 (pp. 123–84).

81 M. F. K. Fisher, 'The Gastronomical Me' [1943], in *The Art of Eating*, p. 353 (pp. 350–572).

82 Orwell, *Down and Out*, pp. 80–1.

83 Bowker, *George Orwell*, p. 147.

84 Ibid., p. 148.

85 Joseph Roth, 'Der alte Kellner' [1929], in *Panoptikum*, pp. 49–52.

86 Ernest Hemingway, 'A Clean, Well-Lighted Place', in Ernest Hemingway, *Winner Take Nothing* (New York: Scribner, 1933), pp. 17–24.

87 Roth, 'Der alte Kellner', p. 51.

88 André Zwiers, 'Friedrich Hussong – Die dunkle Seite des Weimarer Journalismus', in Ulrich P. Schäfer, Thomas Schiller and Georg Schütte (eds), *Journalismus in Theorie und Praxis: Beiträge zur universitären Journalistenausbildung* (Konstanz: UVK, 1999), pp. 39–60.

89 Friedrich Hussong, *Der Tisch der Jahrhunderte* (Berlin: Brunnen, 1937), p. 145.

90 Orwell, *Down and Out*, p. 79.

91 Ibid., pp. 68–9.

92 Gerta Pfeffer, 'Ich hätte gerne mitgetanzt', in Margarete Limberg and Hubert Rübsaat (eds), *Sie durften nicht mehr Deutsche sein: Jüdischer Alltag in Selbstzeugnissen 1933–1938* (Frankfurt: Campus, 1990), pp. 140–2. Pfeffer managed to emigrate to Great Britain (*Sie durften nicht mehr Deutsche sein*, p. 368).

93 Orwell, *Down and Out*, pp. 118–21; George Orwell, *The Road to Wigan Pier* [1937] (London: Penguin, 2014), p. 20.

94 David Grünspecht, 'Ein Viehhändler gibt auf', in *Sie durften nicht mehr Deutsche sein*, pp. 118–21; on the garlic insult: Marion A. Kaplan,

Between Dignity and Despair: Jewish Life in Nazi Germany (New York: Oxford University Press, 1998), pp. 34–5.

95 Joseph Wechsberg, *Visum für Amerika* (Moravian Ostrava: Kittl, 1939), p. 60.

96 Wechsberg, *Visum für Amerika*, p. 91.

97 Susanne Kippenberger, *Am Tisch: Die kulinarische Bohème oder die Entdeckung der Lebenslust* (Berlin: Bloomsbury, 2012), p. 113.

98 Wechsberg, *Visum für Amerika*, pp. 71–2.

99 *Die Tagebücher von Joseph Goebbels*, Part I: *Aufzeichnungen 1923–1941*; volume 8: *April–November 1940*, ed. Jana Richter (Munich: Saur, 1998), pp. 382–4; 388.

100 *Die Tagebücher von Joseph Goebbels*, Part I; volume 5, p. 390.

101 *Die Tagebücher von Joseph Goebbels*, Part I; volume 6, p. 182.

102 *Die Tagebücher von Joseph Goebbels*, Part I; volume 8, pp. 382–4; 388.

103 Patric Kuh, *The Last Days of Haute Cuisine* (New York: Penguin, 2001), pp. 7–16; Thomas McNamee, *The Man Who Changed the Way We Eat: Craig Claiborne and the American Food Renaissance* (New York: Free Press, 2012), pp. 80–1.

104 Jean-Paul Sartre, *Being and Nothingness* (New York: Washington Square Press, 1992), trans. Hazel E. Barnes, p. 101.

105 Christa Hackenesch, *Jean-Paul Sartre* (Reinbek: Rowohlt, 2001), pp. 60–4.

106 Sartre, *Being and Nothingness*, p. 672.

107 Ibid., pp. 101–2.

108 Peter J. Atkins, 'Communal Feeding in War Time: British Restaurants, 1940–1947', in Ina Zweiniger-Bargielowska, Rachel Duffett and Alain Drouard (eds), *Food and War in Twentieth Century Europe* (Farnham: Ashgate, 2011), pp. 139–53.

109 According to Sartre the 'first act of bad faith is to flee what it cannot flee, to flee what it is' (*Being and Nothingness*, p. 115).

110 Sartre, *Being and Nothingness*, pp. 101–2. On the ambiguity of the waiter figure, see D. Z. Phillips, 'Bad Faith and Sartre's Waiter', in *Philosophy* 56/251 (1981): 30 (23–31).

111 William Foote Whyte, *Participant Observer: An Autobiography* (Ithaca, NY: ILR, 1994), p. 150.

112 Whyte, *Human Relations in the Restaurant Industry* (New York: McGraw Hill, 1948), p. 128.

113 Ibid., p. 115; Kurent, *Frances R. Donovan and the Chicago School of Sociology*, p. 106.

2. POSTWAR HUNGER

1 James Baldwin, 'Notes of a Native Son' [1955], in James Baldwin, *Notes of a Native Son* (London: Corgi, 1974), pp. 78–9 (pp. 71–95).

2 The topic of the sketches and discussions is a coffee house, not a

restaurant. Joseph Wechsberg, 'Simon Wiesenthal – Der Mann und seine Aufgabe', in Simon Wiesenthal, *Doch die Mörder leben*, ed. Joseph Wechsberg (Munich: Droemer Knaur, 1987), pp. 56–8 (pp. 7–58).

3 Wolfram Siebeck, *Das Haar in der Suppe habe ich nicht bestellt: Erinnerungen eines Berufsessers* (Frankfurt: Eichborn, 1992), pp. 54–67.

4 Tony Judt, *Postwar: A History of Europe Since 1945* (London: Penguin, 2005).

5 Siebeck, *Das Haar in der Suppe*, pp. 54–67.

6 George Cotkin, *Existential America* (Baltimore, NJ: Johns Hopkins University Press, 2003), pp. 100–2.

7 Baldwin, 'Notes of a Native Son', pp. 80–1.

8 Joseph Wechsberg, *Blue Trout, Black Truffles: The Peregrinations of an Epicure* (New York: Knopf, 1953), pp. 70–82.

9 Siebeck, *Das Haar in der Suppe*, pp. 86–8.

10 Baldwin, 'Notes of a Native Son', p. 81. Thoughts on a 'no longer white' world are from Baldwin's essay 'Stranger in the Village' (*Notes of a Native Son*, pp. 135–49).

11 Jacques Pépin, *The Apprentice: My Life in the Kitchen* (Boston, MA: Houghton Mifflin, 2003), pp. 46–50.

12 Erving Goffman, *The Presentation of Self in Everyday Life* [1959], (Harmondsworth: Penguin, 1969), pp. 118–20; Gary Alan Fine and Philip Manning, 'Erving Goffman', in *The Blackwell Companion to Major Social Theorists*, ed. George Ritzer (Malden, MA.: Blackwell, 2003), pp. 457–85.

13 Pépin, *The Apprentice*, pp. 76–103.

14 Vera Hierholzer, 'Wie die Pizza nach Deutschland kam', in Corinna Engel, Helmut Gold and Rosemarie Wesp (eds), *Satt: Kochen, Essen, Reden* (Heidelberg: Edition Braus, 2009), pp. 56–7.

15 Maren Möhring, *Fremdes Essen: Die Geschichte der ausländischen Gastronomie in der Bundesrepublik Deutschland* (Munich: Oldenbourg, 2012), p. 466 (cf. pp. 235–312).

16 Hierholzer, 'Wie die Pizza nach Deutschland kam', pp. 56–7; appraisal in *Die Küche*: cited in Möhring, *Fremdes Essen*, pp. 251.

17 Thomas McNamee, *The Man Who Changed the Way We Eat*, p. 48; Craig Claiborne, *A Feast Made for Laughter: A Memoir with Recipes* (Garden City, NY: Doubleday, 1982), pp. 120–2.

18 Gael Greene, *Insatiable: Tales from a Life of Delicious Excess* (New York: Grand Central, 2006), pp. 7–10; 58.

19 Alfred Kölling, *Fachbuch für Kellner: Theorie und Praxis im Kellnerberuf* [1956] (Leipzig: Fachbuchverlag, 1958), pp. 16; 203–12.

20 Pépin, *The Apprentice*, pp. 134–46.

21 Sasha Issenberg, *The Sushi Economy: Globalization and the Making of a Modern Delicacy* (New York: Gotham, 2007), pp. xi; 71–5.

22 Issenberg, *The Sushi Economy*, p. 240.

23 Siebeck, *Das Haar in der Suppe*, pp. 106–7.

24 Owen Edwards, 'Courage at the Greensboro Lunch Counter', in

Smithsonian Magazine (February 2010), available online at: <http://www. smithsonianmag.com/arts-culture/courage-at-the-greensboro-lunch-counter-4507661/?no-ist> (accessed October 2015); Taylor Branch, *Parting the Waters: America in the King Years, 1954–1963* (New York: Touchstone, 1988), pp. 270–5.

25 Ulrich Herbert, *Geschichte Deutschlands im 20. Jahrhundert* (Munich: Beck, 2014), pp. 761–3.

26 Michael Bock, 'Metamorphosen der Vergangenheitsbewältigung', in Clemens Albrecht, Günter Behrmann and Michael Bock (eds), *Die intellektuelle Gründung der Bundesrepublik: Eine Wirkungsgeschichte der Frankfurter Schule* (Frankfurt: Campus, 1999), pp. 558–9 (pp. 530–66).

27 Michael Koetzle, 'Die Zeitschrift *twen*: Revision einer Legende', in Michael Koetzle (ed.), *Die Zeitschrift* twen: *Revision einer Legende* (Munich: Klinkhardt und Biermann, 1995), pp. 16, 53 (pp. 12–73).

28 Wolfram Siebeck, 'Fleckhaus, der Guru: Eine Erinnerung', in *Die Zeitschrift* twen, pp. 234–6; on Siebeck's significance in the history of German food culture: Kippenberger, *Am Tisch*, pp. 92–107.

29 Iwan Morgan, 'The New Movement: The Student Sit-Ins in 1960', in Iwan Morgan and Philip Davies (eds), *From Sit-Ins to SNCC: The Student Civil Rights Movement in the 1960s* (Gainesville, FL: University Press of Florida, 2012,) p. 8 (pp. 1–22). Counter restaurants in urban centres were cleverly selected locations for the protest movement. They were a gathering place for both black and white customers, while in many other restaurants this was not the case due to geographic segregation (Andrew Hurley, *Diners, Bowling Alleys, and Trailer Parks: Chasing the American Dream in Postwar Consumer Culture* (New York: Basic, 2001), p. 90. The 1930s civil rights protests of students in the traditionally African American Howard University in the segregated restaurants of the American Congress building were explored early on by Elliott M. Rudwick in his essay 'Oscar De Priest and the Jim Crow Restaurant in the U. S. House of Representatives' (in *The Journal of Negro Education* 35/1 [1966],: 77–82).

30 Edwards, 'Courage at the Greensboro Lunch Counter'; Branch, *Parting the Waters*, pp. 270–5.

31 McNamee, *The Man Who Changed the Way We Eat*, p. 83.

32 David Morowitz, 'Introduction', in David Morowitz (ed.), *Trifles Make Perfection: The Selected Essays of Joseph Wechsberg* (Jaffrey, NH: David R. Godine, 1999), pp. vii–x.

33 Mary F. Corey, *The World Through a Monocle: The New Yorker at Midcentury* (Cambridge, MA: Harvard University Press, 1999), pp. 14–15; 63.

34 Joseph Wechsberg, *Dining at the Pavillon* (Boston, MA: Little, Brown and Company, 1962), pp. 204–6.

35 Anne Moody, *Coming of Age in Mississippi* (New York: Dial, 1968), pp. 235–40. White activists also took part in the protests in Jackson:

see John R. Salter, *Jackson, Mississippi: An American Chronicle of Struggle and Schism* (Hicksville, NY: Exposition, 1979).

36 Holger Uske, *Rolf Anschütz und das Japanrestaurant Suhl* (Suhl: Stadtverwaltung, 2012, pp. 20–1).

37 Karin Falkenberg, *Der 'Waffenschmied' in Suhl: Das einzige Japan-Restaurant der DDR. Ein Jahrhundert Firmengeschichte* (Würzburg: Institut für Alltagskultur, 2000), pp. 19–38.

38 Cited in Falkenberg, *Der 'Waffenschmied' in Suhl*, p. 23.

39 Pépin, *The Apprentice*, pp. 155–65.

40 Ibid., pp. 211–12.

41 Thomas McNamee, *Alice Waters and Chez Panisse: The Romantic, Impractical, Often Eccentric, Ultimately Brilliant Making of a Food Revolution* (New York: Penguin, 2007), pp. 2; 41–9.

42 George Packer, *The Unwinding: An Inner History of the New America* (New York: Farrar, Straus and Giroux, 2013), pp. 184–9.

43 Henry Chesbrough, Sohyeong Kim and Alice Agogino, 'Chez Panisse: Building an Open Innovation Ecosystem', in *California Management Review* 56/4 (2014): 144–71.

44 McNamee, *Alice Waters*, p. 59.

45 Jean-Philippe Derenne, 'Nouvelle Cuisine', in *Encyclopedia of Food and Culture*, ed. Solomon Katz (New York: Scribner, 2003), p. 569 (pp. 569–72).

46 McNamee, *The Man Who Changed the Way We Eat*, pp. 191–3.

47 Derenne, 'Nouvelle Cuisine', pp. 569–72; Rambourg, *Histoire de la cuisine et de la gastronomie françaises*, p. 298.

48 McNamee, *The Man Who Changed the Way We Eat*, p. 196.

49 Greene, *Insatiable*, pp. 161–3.

50 Paczensky/Dünnebier, *Kulturgeschichte des Essens und Trinkens*, p. 522.

51 McNamee, *The Man Who Changed the Way We Eat*, p.193.

52 Nigel Slater, *Toast: The Story of a Boy's Hunger* (London: Harper Perennial, 2003), pp. 189–200.

53 Katherine G. Bristol's ambivalent evaluation in her essay 'The Pruitt-Igoe Myth', in *Journal of Architectural Education* 44/3 (1991): 163–71.

54 Eric Darton, 'The Janus Face of Architectural Terrorism: Minoru Yamasaki, Mohammed Atta, and Our World Trade Center', in Michael Sorkin and Sharon Zukin (eds), *After the World Trade Center: Rethinking New York City* (New York: Routledge, 2002), pp. 88, 92 (pp. 87–130).

55 Andrew Ross, 'The Odor of Publicity', in *After the World Trade Center*, pp. 122–3 (pp. 121–30).

56 Eric Darton, *Divided We Stand: A Biography of New York's World Trade Center* (New York: Basic, 1999), pp. 153–4.

57 Gael Greene, 'The Most Spectacular Restaurant in the World', in *New York* (31 May 1976), available online at: <http://www.insatiable-critic.com/Article.aspx?id= 1322&AspxAutoDetectCookieSupport=1> (accessed October 2015).

58 Steven Greenhouse, 'Windows on the World Workers Say Their Boss Didn't Do Enough', in the *New York Times* (4 June 2002), available online at: <http://www.nytimes.com/2002/06/04/ nyregion/windows-on-the-world-workers-say-their-boss-didn-t-do-enough.html> (accessed October 2015).

59 Truman Capote, *Answered Prayers: The Unfinished Novel* (London: Hamish Hamilton, 1986), pp. 141–81.

60 Falkenberg, *Der 'Waffenschmied' in Suhl*, p. 27.

61 Gerald Clarke, *Capote: A Biography* (New York: Simon & Schuster, 2010), pp. 462–73; A somewhat varying account (for example with regards to the Woodward suicide) can be found in George Plimpton, *Truman Capote: In Which Various Friends, Enemies, Acquaintances, and Detractors Recall His Turbulent Career* (New York: Doubleday, 1997), pp. 337–55.

62 Jefferson Cowie, *Stayin' Alive: The 1970s and the Last Days of the Working Class* (New York: New Press, 2010), pp. 12–13.

63 Claiborne, *Feast*, p. 225; McNamee, *The Man Who Changed the Way We Eat*, pp. 202–11.

64 Gerald Mars and Michael Nicod, *The World of Waiters* (London: Allen & Unwin, 1984), pp. 2, 10.

65 Ibid., pp. 12–13.

66 Ibid., p. 16.

67 Ibid., p. 99.

68 Ibid., p. 12.

69 Wolfram Siebeck, 'Küchenstar-Parade: Was Frankreichs beste Köche anrichteten', in *Die Zeit* (27 October 1978); Wolfram Siebeck, '... und die Äpfel von der faden Sorte: Essen im Maxim's, nachdem es einen Stern und einen Türhüter verlor', in *Die Zeit* (28 April 1978); Wolfgang Lechner, 'Schickt Siebeck auf den Mars!', in *Die Zeit* (21 September 2008); Wolfram Siebeck, 'Der Sauerbraten war ein Schock: Aber der Blick aus dem Speisewagen war herrlich', in *Die Zeit* (28 November 1975); Wolfram Siebeck, 'Mit deutscher Zunge: Jetzt weiß ich, wie ein deutscher Lyriker in Würzburg schlemmt', in *Die Zeit* (23. May 1975); Wolfram Siebeck, 'Weg mit der Mehlschwitze!', in *Die Zeit* (15 March 1985); All articles are available online at <www.zeit.de>.

70 Greene, 'The Most Spectacular Restaurant in the World'.

71 Cited in Darton, *Divided We Stand*, p. 154.

72 Greene, 'The Most Spectacular Restaurant in the World'.

73 Doris Witt, *Black Hunger: Soul Food and America* (Minneapolis, MN: University of Minnesota Press, 2004), pp. 58–9.

74 Mimi Sheraton, *Eating My Words: An Appetite for Life* (New York: Harper, 2006), pp. 22–6; McNamee, *The Man Who Changed the Way We Eat*, pp. 218–19.

75 N.N., 'Who's Killing the Great Chefs of France? Mimi Sheraton Proves They Dish It Out But Can't Take It', in *People* (17 December

1979), available online at: <http://www.people.com/ people/archive/ article/0„2007345,00.html> (accessed October 2015).

76 Ray Kroc, *Grinding It Out: The Making of McDonald's* (New York: St Martin's Press, 1982), pp. 163–5.

77 Cited in Hogan, *Selling 'em by the Sack*, pp. 148–51.

78 McNamee, *Alice Waters*, p. 176.

79 Ibid., pp. 170–1.

80 Christopher Alexander, Sara Ishikawa and Murray Silverstein, *A Pattern Language: Towns, Buildings, Constructions* (New York: Oxford University Press, 1977), pp. 444–7.

81 McNamee, *Alice Waters*, pp. 166–72.

82 Alexander/Ishikawa/Silverstein, *A Pattern Language*, pp. 847–51.

83 Arlie Hochschild, *The Managed Heart: Commercialization of Human Feeling* [1983] (Berkeley. CA: University of California Press, 2003), p. ix.

84 Hochschild, *The Managed Heart*, p. 105.

85 Ibid., pp. 198–200.

86 Cameron Lynne Macdonald and Carmen Sirianni, 'The Service Society and the Changing Experience of Work', in Cameron Lynne Macdonald and Carmen Sirianni (eds), *Working in the Service Society* (Philadelphia, PA: Temple University Press, 1996), p. 3 (pp. 1–26).

87 Falkenberg, *Der 'Waffenschmied' in Suhl*, pp. 43–4.

88 Uske, *Rolf Anschütz und das Japanrestaurant Suhl*, pp. 47–50.

3. THE PRESENT DAY

1 John Burnett, *England Eats Out: A Social History of Eating Out in England from 1830 to the Present* (Harlow: Pearson Longman, 2004), p. 307.

2 Heston Blumenthal, *The Fat Duck Cookbook* (London: Bloomsbury, 2009), pp. 17–30.

3 Colman Andrews, *Ferran: The Inside Story of El Bulli and the Man Who Reinvented Food* (New York: Gotham, 2011), pp. 51–67.

4 Robin Leidner, *Fast Food, Fast Talk: Service Work and the Routinization of Everyday Life* (Berkeley, CA: University of California Press, 1993), pp. 54–60.

5 Andrews, *Ferran*, pp. 85–6.

6 Leidner, *Fast Food, Fast Talk*, pp. 60–72.

7 Andrews, *Ferran*, pp. 110–33.

8 Melinda Nadj Abonji, *Tauben fliegen auf* (Salzburg: Jung und Jung, 2010), English: Melinda Nadj Abonji, *Fly Away, Pigeon*, translated by Tess Lewis (London: Seagull Books/ University of Chicago Press, 2015), pp. 56, 68, 71.

9 Leidner, *Fast Food, Fast Talk*, pp. 72–82, 226–31.

10 Abonji, *Fly Away, Pigeon*, pp. 189, 190, 198.

11 Anthony Bourdain, 'Don't Eat Before Reading This: A New York Chef Spills Some Trade Secrets', in *The New Yorker* (19 April 1999), available online at: <http://www.newyorker.com/ magazine/1999/04/19/ dont-eat-before-reading-this> (accessed October 2015).

12 Blumenthal, *The Fat Duck Cookbook*, pp. 67–91; Maria-José Oruna-Concha, Lisa Methven, Heston Blumenthal, Christopher Young and Donald S. Mottram, 'Differences in Glutamic Acid and 5'-Ribonucleotide Contents between Flesh and Pulp of Tomatoes and the Relationship with Umami Taste', in *Journal of Agricultural and Food Chemistry* 55/14 (2007): 5776–80.

13 Joe L. Kincheloe, *The Sign of the Burger: McDonald's and the Culture of Power*, (Philadelphia, PA: Temple University Press, 2002), p. 1; Paul Ariès and Christian Terras, *José Bové: La révolte d'un paysan* (Villeurbane: Éditions Golias, 2000).

14 Anthony Bourdain, *Kitchen Confidential: Adventures in the Culinary Underbelly* (London: Bloomsbury, 2000), pp. 22–4, 108–9, 300–3.

15 Barbara Ehrenreich, *Nickel and Dimed: On (Not) Getting By in America* (New York: Holt, 2001), pp. 220–1.

16 Ehrenreich, *Nickel and Dimed*, pp. 11–49.

17 Harald Großkopf, 'Wallenstein History', available online at: <http://www.haraldgrosskopf.de/wallenstein.html#History> (accessed October 2015).

18 Ehrenreich, *Nickel and Dimed*, pp. 11–49.

19 Saru Jayaraman, *Behind the Kitchen Door* (Ithaca, NY: Cornell University Press, 2009), pp. 159–70.

20 Ehrenreich, *Nickel and Dimed*, pp. 11–49.

21 Jürgen Dollase, 'Was man auf den Silvesterkarten deutscher Restaurants vermisst', in *Frankfurter Allgemeine Zeitung* (29 December 1999), p. 49; Jürgen Dollase, 'Wenn gute Küche an die Nieren geht', in *Frankfurter Allgemeine Zeitung* (27 December 1999), p. 58; Jürgen Dollase, 'Der Fernsehkoch aus der Nähe', in *Frankfurter Allgemeine Zeitung* (14 March 2001), p. 58; Jürgen Dollase, 'Ich bin überall verkehrt, sonst wäre nichts aus mir geworden: Die Gastronomiekritik muss offener und deutlicher werden', in *Frankfurter Allgemeine Zeitung* (18 October 2000), p. 76.

22 Sékou Siby, 'When Moises Rivas Was Hired, I Was Assigned to Train Him', available online at <http://storycorps.org/listen/sekou-siby/> (accessed October 2015).

23 Birgit Mair, *Die Opfer des NSU und die Aufarbeitung der Verbrechen* (Nuremberg: Institut für sozialwissenschaftliche Forschung, Bildung und Beratung, 2013), pp. 16–17.

24 Jayaraman, *Behind the Kitchen Door*, pp. 167–9.

25 Bill Buford, *Heat: An Amateur's Adventures as Kitchen Slave, Line Cook, Pasta-Maker and Apprentice to a Butcher in Tuscany* (New York: Vintage, 2007), pp. 81–90.

26 Mair, *Die Opfer des NSU*, pp. 18–19; Stefan Aust and Dirk Laabs,

Heimatschutz: Der Staat und die Mordserie des NSU (Munich: Pantheon, 2014), pp. 606–7.

27 Buford, *Heat*, pp. 81–90.

28 Fabian Virchow, Tanja Thomas and Elke Grittmann, *'Das Unwort erklärt die Untat': Die Berichterstattung über die NSU-Morde – eine Medienkritik* (Frankfurt: Otto-Brenner-Stiftung, 2014), p. 23.

29 *Unsere Wunden kann die Zeit nicht heilen: Was der NSU-Terror für die Opfer und Angehörigen bedeutet*, ed. Barbara John (Bonn: Bundeszentrale für politische Bildung, 2014), p. 95.

30 Aust/Laabs, *Heimatschutz*, p. 617.

31 Blumenthal, *The Fat Duck Cookbook*, pp. 90–101.

32 Buford, *Heat*, pp. 104–5, 115–16.

33 Ibid., p. 301.

34 Marta Arzak and Josep Maria Pinto, 'Ferran Adrià's Participation in Documenta 12', in Vincente Todol (ed.), *Food for Thought, Thought for Food* (Barcelona: Actar, 2009), pp. 81, 105 (pp. 78–109).

35 Manfred Weber-Lamberdière, *Die Revolutionen des Ferran Adrià: Wie ein Katalane das Kochen zur Kunst machte* (Berlin: Bloomsbury, 2007), p. 174.

36 Noreen Malone, 'Bulli for You', in *Slate* (14.April 2011), available online at: <http://www.slate.com/articles/life/food/2011/04/bulli_for_you.html> (accessed October 2015).

37 Juan Moreno, *Teufelsköche: An den heißesten Herden der Welt* (Munich: Piper, 2011), pp. 14, 116–27, 226–39.

38 Lisa Abend, *The Sorcerer's Apprentices: A Season in the Kitchen at Ferran Adrià's El Bulli* (New York: Free Press, 2011), pp. 65–6, 109–11.

39 Barbara John (ed.), *Unsere Wunden kann die Zeit nicht heilen*, pp. 72–83.

40 A. J. Smith et al., 'A Large Foodborne Outbreak of Norovirus in Diners at a Restaurant in England between January and February 2009', in *Epidemiology and Infection* 140 (2012): 1695–1701; Blumenthal, *The Fat Duck Cookbook*, pp. 144–9; see also the Wikipedia entry for 'Heston Blumenthal' (accessed October 2015).

41 Moreno, *Teufelsköche*, pp. 114–29.

42 Marilyn Hagerty, *Grand Forks: A History of American Dining in 128 Reviews* (New York: Harper Collins, 2013), pp. 2, 228–33.

43 Magnus Nilsson, *Fäviken* (London: Phaidon, 2012), pp. 29–37.

44 Camille Dodero, 'Marilyn Hagerty, Grand Forks Olive Garden Reviewer, Speaks', in *Village Voice* (8 March 2012), available online at <http:// www.villagevoice.com/ restaurants/marilyn-hagerty-grand-forks-olive-garden-reviewer-speaks-6574705> (accessed October 2015); see also the Wikipedia entry for 'Marilyn Hagerty' (accessed October 2015).

45 Hagerty, *Grand Forks*, pp. 233–5.

46 Marten Rolff, 'Schwedenhappen', in *Süddeutsche Zeitung* (26 April 2013), p. 3.

47 Hans Välimäki et al., 'New Nordic Kitchen Manifesto', available online at <http://newnordicfood.org/about-nnf-ii/new-nordic-kitchen-manifesto/> (accessed October 2015).

48 Välimäki; Rolff, p. 3.

49 Julia Moskin, 'New Nordic Cuisine Draws Disciples', in *New York Times* (23 August 2011), available online at <http://www.nytimes.com/2011/08/24/dining/new-nordic-cuisine-draws-disciples.html?_r=0> (accessed 17 August 2015).

50 Nilsson, *Fäviken*, pp. 29–37, 243–8.

51 Kai Strittmatter, 'Er trug seinen Teller mit den eigenen Händen', in *Süddeutsche Zeitung* (27 January 2014), p. 8; Mia Li, 'Divining China's Direction by What Xi Ate', in *New York Times: Sinosphere* (30 December 2013), available online at <http://sinosphere.blogs.nytimes.com/2013/12/30/divining-chinas-direction-by-what-xi-ate/?_r=0> (accessed October 2015).

52 Jayaraman, *Behind the Kitchen Door*, pp. 102–29.

53 Yiyuan Zhou, 'Neuester Image-Coup: Chinas Präsident isst im Straßenlokal', in *Epoch Times* (6 January 2014), available online at <http://www.epochtimes.de/Neuester-Image-Coup-Chinas-Praesident-isst-im-Strassenlokal-a1120622.html> (accessed October 2015).

54 Nilsson, *Fäviken*, pp. 29–37.

4. READING RESTAURANTS

1 Daniel Bell, *The Coming of Post-Industrial Society: A Venture in Social Forecasting* (New York: Basic, 1973), p. 20.

2 For a contemporary evaluation of Bell, see Barry Smart, 'Editor's Introduction: Post-Industrial Society and Information Technology', in *Post-Industrial Society*, vol. I, ed. Barry Smart (London: Sage, 2011), pp. xxi–xliv.

3 Ibid., p. 44.

4 Heinrich August Winkler criticizes Bell's vision as an 'exaggerated' representation: Winkler, *Geschichte des Westens: Vom Kalten Krieg zum Mauerfall* (Munich: Beck, 2014), p. 637.

5 Peter Scholliers, 'Novelty and Tradition: The New Landscape for Gastronomy', in Paul Freedman (ed.), *Food: The History of Taste* (London: Thames and Hudson, 2007), pp. 334–5 (pp. 333–57).

6 Scott Lash and John Urry, *Economies of Signs and Space* (London: Sage, 1994), p. 222.

7 George Ritzer, *The McDonaldization of Society* [1993] (Los Angeles, CA: Pine Forge, 2009). For a nuanced discussion of Max Weber's theories, see Christiane Bender and Hans Graßl, *Arbeiten und Leben in der Dienstleistungsgesellschaft* (Konstanz: UVK, 2004). A lively debate of Ritzer's approach is documented in Barry Smart (ed.), *Resisting McDonaldization* (London: Sage, 1999).

8   Ronnie J. Steinberg and Deborah M. Figart, 'Emotional Labor since *The Managed Heart*', in *Annals of the American Academy of Political and Social Science* 561 (1999): 8–26.

9   Rebecca Spang, 'Restaurants', in *Encyclopedia of Food and Culture*, vol. III, ed. Solomon Katz (New York: Scribner, 2003), p. 184 (pp. 179–86).

10 Winfried Speitkamp, *Der Rest ist für Sie! Kleine Geschichte des Trinkgeldes* (Stuttgart: Philipp Reclam, 2008), pp. 9–10; and from a cultural anthropological perspective, David Sutton, 'Tipping: An Anthropological Meditation', in David Beriss and David Sutton (eds), *The Restaurants Book: Ethnographies of Where We Eat* (Oxford: Berg, 2007), pp. 191–204; from an economical perspective, Ofer Azar, 'Do People Tip Because of Psychological or Strategic Motivations? An Empirical Analysis of Restaurant Tipping', in *Applied Economics* 42/23 (2010):3039–44.

11 Katherine S. Newman's excellent ethnographic study, *No Shame in My Game: The Working Poor in the Inner City* (New York: Knopf, 1999), emphasizes how the apparent absence of work ethic amongst the 'working poor' is deceptive.

12 Jordan Weissmann, 'The Fast-Food Strikes Have Been a Stunning Success for Organized Labor', in *Slate* (7 September 2014), available online at <http://www.slate.com/blogs/ moneybox/2014/09/07/the_fast_food_strikes_a_stunning_success_for_organized_labor.html> (accessed October 2015); William Finnegan, 'Dignity: Fast-Food Workers and a New Form of Labor Activism', in *The New Yorker* (15 September 2014), available online at <http://www.newyorker.com/magazine/2014/09/15/dignity-4> (accessed October 2015).

13 Luc Boltanski and Ève Chiapello, *The New Spirit of Capitalism* [1999] (London: Verso, 2005).

14 For a historical and sociological exploration of service work in the restaurant, see Cameron Lynne Macdonald and Carmen Sirianni (eds), *Working in the Service Society* (Philadelphia, PA: Temple University Press, 1996), especially Greta Foff Paules, 'Resisting the Symbolism of Service among Waitresses', pp. 264–90; also Greta Foff Paules, *Dishing It Out: Power and Resistance among Waitresses in a New Jersey Restaurant* (Philadelphia, PA: Temple University Press, 1991); and, a little further removed from the more precise definition of the restaurant, but still a rewarding read: Kim Pryce-Glinn, *Strip Club: Gender, Power, and Sex Work* (New York: New York University Press, 2010), as well as James P. Spradley and Brenda J. Mann, *The Cocktail Waitress: Women's Work in a Man's World* (New York: Knopf, 1975); Dorothy Sue Cobble presents a socio-historical study of unionized American waitresses in *Dishing It Out: Waitresses and Their Unions in the Twentieth Century* (Urbana, IL: University of Illinois Press, 1992); on the cultural and social history of the waitress: Alison Owings, *Hey Waitress! The USA from the Other Side of the Tray* (Berkeley, CA:

University of California Press, 2004); on early attempts to unionize (male) black American waiters: Margaret Garb, 'The Great Chicago Waiters' Strike: Producing Urban Space, Organizing Labor, Challenging Racial Divides in 1890s Chicago', in *Journal of Urban History* 40/6 (2014): 1079–98; on the history of professional female chefs: Ann Cooper, *'A Woman's Place is in the Kitchen': The Evolution of Women Chefs* (New York: Van Nostrand, 1998).

15 Jean-Pierre Hassoun, 'Restaurants dans la ville-monde: Douceurs et amertumes', in *Ethnologie Française* 44/1 (2014): 6 (5–10).

16 On the significance of marked, scarred and scratched hands in the depiction of restaurant workers: Simon Wroe's novel *Chop Chop* (London: Penguin, 2014), pp. 32–3.

17 Gary Alan Fine, *Kitchens: The Culture of Restaurant Work* (Berkeley, CA: University of California Press, 1996), pp. 206–7.

18 Of interest here, Richard Sennett's reflections on Chinese top chefs and their knife techniques: Sennett, *The Craftsman* (London: Penguin, 2008), pp. 165–8.

19 Matthew Crawford, *The World Beyond Your Head: On Becoming an Individual in an Age of Distraction* (New York: Farrar, 2015), pp. 32–5.

20 An excellent case study: Karla A. Erickson, 'Tight Spaces and Salsa-Stained Aprons: Bodies at Work in American Restaurants', in David Beriss and David Sutton (eds), *The Restaurants Book: Ethnographies of Where We Eat* (Oxford: Berg, 2007), pp. 17–23. A more comprehensive study: Karla A. Erickson, *The Hungry Cowboy: Service and Community in a Neighborhood Restaurant* (Jackson, MS: University Press of Mississippi, 2009).

21 Jayaraman, *Behind the Kitchen Door*; Elvire Camus, 'Violences en cuisine: les vieilles traditions ont la vie dure', in *Le Monde* (29 November 2014), available online at: <http://www.lemonde.fr/m-styles/article/2014/ 11/29/violences-en-cuisine-les-vieilles-traditions-ont-la-vie-dure_453156 0_4497319.html> (accessed October 2015); David Shipler, *The Working Poor: Invisible in America* (New York: Vintage, 2004), pp. 19–20.

22 Lizabeth Cohen, *A Consumer's Republic: The Politics of Mass Consumption in Postwar America* (New York: Knopf, 2003), p. 404.

23 Alison Pearlman, *Smart Casual: The Transformation of Gourmet Restaurant Style in America* (Chicago, IL: University of Chicago Press, 2013), pp. 86–7.

24 See Charlotte Biltekoff, *Eating Right in America: The Cultural Politics of Food and Health* (Durham, NC: Duke University Press, 2013).

25 Adam Gopnik, *The Table Comes First: Family, France, and the Meaning of Food* (New York: Vintage, 2012), pp. 4–5.

26 Michael Pollan, *Cooked: A Natural History of Transformation* (London: Penguin, 2013), pp. 3–7.

27 From an urbanist perspective, whilst also taking the function of gastronomy into consideration: Sharon Zukin, *Naked City: The Death*

and Life of Authentic Urban Places (Oxford: Oxford University Press, 2011), pp. xii–xiii.

28 Peter Naccarato and Kathleen LeBesco, *Culinary Capital* (London: Berg, 2012), p. 9; by way of example: Michael Pollan, *Omnivore's Dilemma: A Natural History of Four Meals* (New York: Penguin, 2006), and Jonathan Safran Foer, *Eating Animals* (Boston, MA: Little, Brown and Company, 2009).

29 Carlo Petrini, *Slow Food Nation: Why Our Food Should Be Good, Clean, and Fair* (New York: Rizzoli Ex Libris, 2013), p. 375.

30 James L. Watson and Melissa L. Caldwell, 'Introduction', in James L. Watson and Melissa L. Caldwell (eds), *The Cultural Politics of Food and Eating: A Reader* (Malden, MA: Blackwell, 2005), p. 3 (pp. 1–10).

31 On the demise of French haute cuisine: Patric Kuh, *The Last Days of Haute Cuisine* (New York: Penguin, 2001).

32 David Inglis and Debra Gimlin, 'Food Globalizations: Ironies and Ambivalences of Food, Cuisine, and Globality', in David Inglis and Debra Gimlin (eds), *The Globalization of Food* (Oxford: Berg, 2010), pp. 14–15 (pp. 3–42).

33 Petrini, *Slow Food Nation*, 2013, p. 56.

34 Amy B. Trubek, *The Taste of Place: A Cultural Journey into Terroir* (Berkeley, CA: University of California Press, 2009), pp. 141–2. Rachel Laudan conducts a polemical analysis of these often nostalgic culinary concepts in 'A Plea for Culinary Modernism: Why We Should Love New, Fast, Processed Food', in *Gastronomica* 1 (2001): 36–44.

35 Valeria Siniscalchi, 'La politique dans l'assiette: Restaurants et restaurateurs dans le mouvement Slow Food en Italie', in *Ethnologie Française* 44/1 (2014): 79 (73–84).

36 For an interpretation of early American gourmets and their niche culture, see David Strauss, *Setting the Table for Julia Child: Gourmet Dining in America, 1934–1961* (Baltimore, MD: Johns Hopkins University Press, 2011).

37 Steven Poole, 'Let's Start the Foodie Backlash', in the *Guardian* (28 September 2012), available online at <http://www.theguardian.com/books/2012/sep/28/lets-start-foodie-backlash> (accessed October 2015); for a differentiated account of the foodie movement, see Josée Johnston and Shyon Baumann, *Foodies: Democracy and Distinction in the Gourmet Foodscape* (New York: Routledge, 2010).

38 Andreas Reckwitz, *The Invention of Creativity: Modern Society and the Culture of the New* (Cambridge: Polity, 2017).

39 Amy B. Trubek, 'The Chef', in *Encyclopedia of Food and Culture*, vol. I, ed. Solomon Katz (New York: Scribner, 2003), pp. 364–6. Autobiographical accounts from the restaurant are numerous in the late twentieth and early twenty-first centuries. It is no coincidence that the following two trends overlap in Western industrial nations: the appetite for the life story of an individual, offered as a model or anti-model for its readers, and the steadily growing interest in

food, its preparation, and the fascinating secrets which are associated with the restaurant as a location. In America, Anthony Bourdain's *Kitchen Confidential* is groundbreaking for its representation of the gastronomic scene as a close-knit society and the kitchen as a location of authentic emotions: stress, sex, violence: *Kitchen Confidential: Adventures in the Culinary Underbelly* (London: Bloomsbury, 2000); In a less romanticized depiction than Bourdain's, located in a chain restaurant and focusing on the social and political context of system gastronomy, Tracie McMillan reports from an Applebee's branch in Brooklyn, yet finds a similar sense of community to that celebrated by Bourdain: *The American Way of Eating: Undercover at Walmart, Applebee's, Farm Fields and the Dinner Table* (New York: Scribner, 2012). The English top chefs tackle even greater issues: Marco Pierre White represents himself as a working-class hero in his autobiography *The Devil in the Kitchen* (London: Orion, 2006) in an attempt to bring himself closer to his readers – in actual fact, his book can be read as a justification for an authoritative style of leadership, for example when he uses axioms such as 'discipline is born out of fear' (p. 150). Gordon Ramsay's *Humble Pie: My Autobiography* is a further product of this genre, assuring its readers that 'there's no place for mummy's boys in a kitchen' (London: Harper, 2007), p. 191. For an antidote to these displays of culinary masculinity, see the highly recommended – and perhaps most interesting from a literary perspective – kitchen autobiography of Gabrielle Hamilton, the owner of the restaurant Prune in New York's East Village. Telling her story, she brings to life the dream of a restaurant as an idealized site of simple pleasures just as vividly as she does the disgusting side of gastronomic work and the stress associated with it (Hamilton describes a maggot-ridden rat carcass, then immediately cuts to the limousine which is chauffeuring her to an appearance on the *Martha Stewart Show*). See *Blood, Bones, and Butter: The Inadvertent Education of a Reluctant Chef* (New York: Random House, 2012), pp. 138–40). Hamilton's story is outstanding because it is written exceptionally well. The chef biography format, however, is now part of the marketing package, which consists not just of the respective chef's restaurant itself but also cookbooks, television appearances and other media presence; for a collection of chef biographies, also part of this package (as the accompanying volume to an American television series), but nonetheless with a less mythologizing perspective on the careers of contemporary head chefs, see Dorothy Hamilton and Patric Kuh (eds), *Chef's Story: 27 Chefs Talk about What Got Them into the Kitchen* (New York: Harper Collins, 2007).

40 Jacques Pépin, *The Apprentice: My Life in the Kitchen* (Boston, MA: Houghton Mifflin, 2003).

41 Jean-Philippe Derenne, 'Nouvelle Cuisine', in *Encyclopedia of Food and Culture*, ed. Solomon Katz (New York: Scribner), pp. 569–72.

42 Rick Bayless's restaurants in Chicago, for example, are known in the early twenty-first century as the go-to destinations for supposedly authentic Mexican cuisine. The contemporary top chef, who has no Mexican roots, acquired his training in a graduate programme for anthropological linguistics – it was, in fact, an academic exploration of Mexican folk culture which led him to gastronomy. However, Bayless also cites other biographical motivating factors: 'I'm the fourth generation in a family of food people' (*Chef's Story*, p. 33).

43 Cailein Gillespie, *European Gastronomy into the 21st Century* (Oxford: Butterworth Heinemann, 2001), p. 164.

44 Joanne Finkelstein, 'Rich Food: McDonald's and Modern Life', in Barry Smart (ed.), *Resisting McDonaldization* (London: Sage, 1999), p. 79 (pp. 70–82). On the crisis of the McDonald's group: Beth Kowitt, 'Fallen Arches: Can McDonald's Get Its Mojo Back?', in *Fortune* (12 November 2014), available online at <http://fortune.com/2014/11/12/can-mcdonalds-get-its-mojo-back/> (accessed October 2015).

45 H. G. Parsa, John T. Self, David Nijite and Tiffany King, 'Why Restaurants Fail', in *Cornell Hotel and Restaurant Administration Quarterly* 46/3 (2005):315 (304–22).

46 Alois Wierlacher, 'Koch und Köchin als Kulturstifter', in Alois Wierlacher and Regina Bendix (eds), *Kulinaristik: Forschung – Lehre – Praxis* (Berlin: LIT, 2008), p. 375 (pp. 358–78).

47 Jürgen Dollase, *Kulinarische Intelligenz* (Wiesbaden: Tre Torri, 2006).

48 Karl R. Popper, *The Open Society and Its Enemies, vol. I: The Spell of Plato* [1944] (London: Routledge, 2002), p. 191.

49 Alice P. Julier, 'Meals: "Eating In" and "Eating Out"', in Anne Murcott, Warren Belasco and Peter Jackson (eds), *The Handbook of Food Research* (London: Bloomsbury, 2013), pp. 339, 342 (pp. 338–51).

50 Popper, *The Open Society*, 2002, p. 218.

51 Spang, 'Restaurants', p. 180.

52 On this vision of the restaurant: Kuh, *Last Days of Haute Cuisine*, p. 213.

53 For a description of an event of this kind – in Aspen, Colorado, 2011 – see Chrystia Freeland, *Plutocrats: The Rise of the New Global Super-Rich and the Fall of Everyone Else* (New York: Penguin, 2012), p. 112.

54 Alexandros Stefanidis, *Beim Griechen: Wie mein Vater in unserer Taverne Geschichte schrieb* (Frankfurt: Fischer, 2010), pp. 252–3.

55 There is a vast amount of literature available on interculturality and the culinary arts. On Chinese restaurants in the United States: Andrew Coe, *Chop Suey: A Cultural History of Chinese Food in the United States* (Oxford: Oxford University Press, 2009); in Canada: Lily Cho, *Eating Chinese: Culture on the Menu in Small-Town Canada* (Toronto: University of Toronto Press, 2010); on the connections between ethnic cuisine and urban development: Annie Hauck-Lawson and Jonathan Deutsch (eds), *Gastropolis: Food and New York City* (New York:

Columbia University Press, 2009). (Martin Manalansan's case study from the neighbourhood of Queens is particularly incisive: 'The Empire of Food: Place, Memory, and Asian "Ethnic Cuisines"', pp. 93–107.) An excellent example of a study with a different geographic focus: Rossella Ceccarini, *Pizza and Pizza Chefs in Japan: A Case of Culinary Globalization* (Leiden: Brill, 2011).

56 Möhring, *Fremdes Essen*, pp. 28–35.

57 Stanley Fish, 'Boutique Multiculturalism, or Why Liberals Are Incapable of Thinking about Hate Speech', in *Critical Inquiry* 23/2 (1997): 378–95.

58 Sharon Zukin, 'Restaurants as "Post-Racial" Spaces: Soul Food and Symbolic Eviction in Bedford-Stuyvesant (Brooklyn)', in *Ethnologie Française* 44/1 (2014): 135–48; Möhring, *Fremdes Essen*, p. 466.

59 Jeffrey M. Pilcher, *Planet Taco: A Global History of Mexican Food* (Oxford: Oxford University Press, 2012), p. 17. A concrete case study about the negotiation of authenticity in ethnic restaurants can be found in Jennie Germann Molz, 'Tasting an Imagined Thailand: Authenticity and Culinary Tourism in Thai Restaurants', in Lucy M. Long (ed.), *Culinary Tourism* (Lexington, KY: University Press of Kentucky, 2004), pp. 53–75.

60 Panikos Panayi, *Spicing Up Britain: The Multicultural History of British Food* (London: Reaktion, 2008), pp. 215–16.

61 See, for example, Zachary W. Brewster, Michael Lynn and Shlytia Cocroft, 'Consumer Racial Profiling in U.S. Restaurants: Exploring Subtle Forms of Service Discrimination against Black Diners', in *Sociological Forum* 29/2 (2014): 476–95, and Zachary W. Brewster and Michael Lynn, 'Black–White Earnings Gap among Restaurant Servers: A Replication, Extension, and Exploration of Consumer Racial Discrimination in Tipping', in *Sociological Inquiry* 84/4 (2014): 545–69.

62 Elizabeth Buettner, '"Going for an Indian": South Asian Restaurants and the Limits of Multiculturalism in Britain', in Krishnendu Ray and Tulasi Srinivas (eds), *Curried Cultures: Globalization, Food, and South Asia* (Berkeley, CA: University of California Press, 2012), p. 141 (pp. 143–74).

63 Robert Ji-Song Ku, *Dubious Gastronomy: The Cultural Politics of Eating Asian in the USA* (Honolulu: University of Hawai'i Press, 2014), p. 13.

64 Krishnendu Ray, 'Global Flows, Local Bodies: Dreams of Pakistani Grill in Manhattan', in *Curried Cultures*, p. 176 (pp. 175–95).

65 Spang, 'Restaurants', p. 180.

66 Alfred Kölling, *Fachbuch für Kellner: Theorie und Praxis im Kellnerberuf* (Leipzig: Fachbuchverlag, 1956), p. 5.

67 Elke Jordan and Thomas Kutsch, 'The Lobby Restaurant in Cologne: A New Concept of Social Integration', in Barbara Maria Köhler et al. (eds), *Poverty and Food in Welfare Societies* (Berlin: Edition Sigma, 1997), pp. 300–1 (pp. 298–303).

68 Howard S. Becker, *Art Worlds* [1982] (Berkeley, CA: University of California Press, 2008), p. 36. Becker's interpretation of a collaborative art world, in which the works are produced in a cooperative network instead of by individual genius, is particularly helpful for the understanding of creativity within the sphere of the restaurant.

69 Barbara Santich, 'Restaurant', in *The Oxford Companion to Food*, ed. Alan Davidson (Oxford: Oxford University Press, 2006), p. 661 (pp. 660–1).

70 Andrew P. Haley, *Turning the Tables: Restaurants and the Rise of the American Middle Class, 1880–1920* (Chapel Hill, NC: University of North Carolina Press, 2011), pp. 12–13.

71 Paul Freedman, 'Introduction: A New History of Cuisine', in *Food: A History of Taste,* ed. Paul Freedman (London: Thames & Hudson, 2007), p. 18 (pp. 7–33). A model study on the very concrete transition zone between the culinary and the snack establishment (the 'Profi-Grill' in Bochum-Wattenscheid) can be found in Härtig, 'Immer lecker: Über die Kultur der Pommesbuden im Ruhrgebiet', in Christian F. Hoffstadt et al. (eds), *Gastrosophical Turn: Essen zwischen Medizin und Öffentlichkeit* (Bochum: Projekt, 2009), pp. 43–57.

72 Jürgen Dollase, 'Wenn der Kopf zum Magen kommt: Theoriebildung in der Kochkunst', in Daniele Dell'Agli (ed.), *Essen als ob nicht: Gastrosophische Modelle* (Frankfurt: Suhrkamp, 2009), p. 96 (pp. 67–99).

73 Alois Wierlacher, 'Kulinaristik – Vision und Programm', in *Kulinaristik*, p. 4 (pp. 2–15); on Rousseau and connections with the ethical and political positioning of contemporary gastrosophers: Harald Lemke, 'Genealogie des gastrosophischen Hedonismus', *Essen als ob nicht* (pp. 17–65), and Harald Lemke, *Über das Essen: Philosophische Erkundungen* (Munich: Wilhelm Fink, 2014).

74 Joanne Finkelstein, *Fashioning Appetite: Restaurants and the Making of Modern Identity* (New York: Columbia University Press, 2014); Joanne Finkelstein, *Dining Out: A Sociology of Modern Manners* (New York: New York University Press, 1991).

75 Pierre Bourdieu, *A Social Critique of the Judgement of Taste*, translated by Richard Nice (London: Routledge Classics 2010), p. xxix; in the English-language context: Alan Warde and Lydia Martens, *Eating Out: Social Differentiation, Consumption and Pleasure* (Cambridge: Cambridge University Press, 2000).

76 On distinction practices amongst 'foodies': Johnston/Baumann, *Foodies*.

77 See also Tobias Döring, 'Kulturlabor Küche: Kleiner Arbeitsbericht aus der englischen Literatur', in Gisela Ecker and Claudia Lillge (eds), *Kulturen der Arbeit* (Munich: Wilhelm Fink, 2011), p. 52 (pp. 51–64).

78 David Beriss and David Sutton, 'Restaurants, Ideal Postmodern Institutions', in David Beriss and David Sutton (eds), *The Restaurants Book: Ethnographies of Where We Eat* (Oxford: Berg, 2007), p. 1

(pp. 1–13); also Brenda Gayle Plummer, 'Restaurant Citizens to the Barricades!', in *American Quarterly* 60/1 (2008): 23–31.

79 Hassoun, 'Restaurants dans la ville-monde', p. 10.

80 The waitress autobiography can be identified as a key genre: Debra Ginsberg's *Waiting: The True Confessions of a Waitress* reflects the tension between the waitressing job as a supposedly temporary position and the identity of a woman who serves in the restaurant for decades on end (New York: HarperCollins, 2000). Phoebe Damrosch's *Service Included: Four-Star Secrets of an Eavesdropping Waiter* (New York: William Morrow, 2007) acts, in contrast to Ginsberg's autobiography, more as an introduction to the extreme heights of top gastronomy – seen from the perspective of the waitress as a supposed insider. Steve Dublanica's autobiographical *Waiter Rant*, which arose from an extremely popular blog, is an account of life as a waiter in less elite restaurants. It demonstrates the cynicism and fighting spirit concealed beneath the facade of the service industry. Dublanica's insight into the male waiter's soul opens up a previously unknown area of the often female-coded service work (*Waiter Rant: Thanks for the Tip – Confessions of a Cynical Waiter*, New York: HarperCollins, 2008). Service roles and masculinity are presented in a more nuanced manner by Thomas Mann (*Confessions of Felix Krull, Confidence Man: The Early Years,* New York: Vintage, 1992) and in Alain Claude Sulzer's variations on the theme in his novel *A Perfect Waiter* (London: Bloomsbury, 2008, translated by John Brownjohn). E. A. Maccannon's collection of biographies from the year 1904 offers a fascinating insight into a completely different waiter identity: African American head waiters attribute themselves great authority as 'dining room commanders' – and this in the early twentieth century, while their civil rights were constantly being attacked outside of the restaurant (E. A. Maccannon, *Commanders of the Dining Room: Biographic Sketches and Portraits of Successful Head Waiters*, New York: Gwendolyn, 1904).

81 A more complete picture can be obtained by reading further 'true stories' from the restaurant. The first recommendation is Christophe Blain's graphic novel about head chef Alain Passard and his kitchen, which is orientated around vegetables of the very best quality (Christophe Blain, *In the Kitchen with Alain Passard: Inside the World (and Mind) of a Master Chef,* San Francisco, CA: Chronicle Books LLC, 2013). Passard contributes recipes to the book, but the most significant element is Blain's translation of the creative process and the connection between product and creative thought into graphic art; the chef is partly caricatured as an obsessive genius, and partly portrayed with great admiration. Writers, too, achieve a similar intensity when they conceal themselves behind gastronomic curtains. The silent star of the genre is the American Michael Ruhlman, whose gripping books of reportage from restaurant kitchens and from the Culinary Institute

of America unite loyalty to detail and empathy in their depiction of the life of the cook– between the extreme physical demands of their shifts and the very different demands of the media society (*The Making of a Chef: Mastering Heat at the Culinary Institute of America*, New York: Holt, 1997; *The Soul of a Chef: The Journey Toward Perfection*, New York: Penguin, 2001; *The Reach of a Chef: Professional Cooks in the Age of the Celebrity*, New York: Penguin, 2007). A similar project follows Leslie Brenner's long-term observation of the New York Restaurant, Daniel (*The Fourth Star: Dispatches from Inside Daniel Boulud's Celebrated New York Restaurant*, New York: Three Rivers, 2002). When restaurant critics publish their collected works, they tend to title them as ambitiously as possible. This applies to *The Man Who Ate the World* by Jay Rayner (London: Headline, 2008) as well as Jeffrey Steingarten's *The Man Who Ate Everything* (London: Headline, 1999). (Steingarten's book includes his gripping account of attending the New York Professional Service School, where he carried out training as a waiter.) See also: Frank Bruni's *Born Round: The Secret History of a Full-Time Eater* (New York: Penguin, 2009), and Ruth Reichl: *Garlic and Sapphires: The Secret Life of a Critic in Disguise*, New York: Penguin, 2005).

82 Paul Stoller, *The Taste of Ethnographic Things: The Senses in Anthropology* (Philadelphia, PA: University of Pennsylvania Press, 1989), p. 155.

83 A critique of observers (like Orwell or Ehrenreich) is expressed very pointedly by Carolyn Betensky, who feels that the heroism of the respective narrator actually hinders a creative and result-orientated questioning of social inequality: Carolyn Betensky, 'Princes as Paupers: Pleasure and the Imagination of Powerlessness', in *Cultural Critique* 58 (2004): 153 (129–57); for a comprehensive depiction, see Mark Pittenger, *Class Unknown: Undercover Investigations of American Work and Poverty from the Progressive Era to the Present* (New York: New York University Press, 2012).

84 On a technical level, this book profited greatly from the reading of much discussed montage-style cultural histories from recent years (for example, Hans Ulrich Gumbrecht, *In 1926: Living at the Edge of Time,* Cambridge, MA: Harvard University Press, 1997, and Florian Illies, *1913: Der Sommer des Jahrhunderts*, Frankfurt: Fischer, 2012, available in English as *1913: The Year Before the Storm*, London: The Clerkenwell Press, 2013, translated by Shaun Whiteside and Jamie Lee Searle). My approach, however, was inspired more by John Dos Passos's inimitable *Manhattan Transfer*, in which montage is used both for the dynamic reproduction of modern sensory impressions as well as the representation and reflection of social inequality within a clearly defined space (John Dos Passos, *Manhattan Transfer* [1925], London: Penguin, 1986).

85 David Shields, *Reality Hunger: A Manifesto* (New York: Knopf, 2010), p. 60.

INDEX

PUSHKIN PRESS

Pushkin Press was founded in 1997, and publishes novels, essays, memoirs, children's books—everything from timeless classics to the urgent and contemporary.

Our books represent exciting, high-quality writing from around the world: we publish some of the twentieth century's most widely acclaimed, brilliant authors such as Stefan Zweig, Marcel Aymé, Teffi, Antal Szerb, Gaito Gazdanov and Yasushi Inoue, as well as compelling and award-winning contemporary writers, including Andrés Neuman, Edith Pearlman, Eka Kurniawan, Ayelet Gundar-Goshen and Chigozie Obioma.

Pushkin Press publishes the world's best stories, to be read and read again. To discover more, visit www.pushkinpress.com.

━━━

THE SPECTRE OF ALEXANDER WOLF

GAITO GAZDANOV

'A mesmerising work of literature' Antony Beevor

SUMMER BEFORE THE DARK

VOLKER WEIDERMANN

'For such a slim book to convey with such poignancy the extinction of a generation of "Great Europeans" is a triumph' *Sunday Telegraph*

MESSAGES FROM A LOST WORLD

STEFAN ZWEIG

'At a time of monetary crisis and political disorder… Zweig's celebration of the brotherhood of peoples reminds us that there is another way' *The Nation*

THE EVENINGS

GERARD REVE

'Not only a masterpiece but a cornerstone manqué of modern European literature' Tim Parks, *Guardian*

BINOCULAR VISION
EDITH PEARLMAN

'A genius of the short story' Mark Lawson, *Guardian*

IN THE BEGINNING WAS THE SEA
TOMÁS GONZÁLEZ

'Smoothly intriguing narrative, with its touches of sinister,
Patricia Highsmith-like menace' *Irish Times*

BEWARE OF PITY
STEFAN ZWEIG

'Zweig's fictional masterpiece' *Guardian*

THE ENCOUNTER
PETRU POPESCU

'A book that suggests new ways of looking at the world
and our place within it' *Sunday Telegraph*

WAKE UP, SIR!
JONATHAN AMES

'The novel is extremely funny but it is also sad and
poignant, and almost incredibly clever' *Guardian*

THE WORLD OF YESTERDAY
STEFAN ZWEIG

'*The World of Yesterday* is one of the greatest memoirs of the twentieth
century, as perfect in its evocation of the world Zweig loved, as it is
in its portrayal of how that world was destroyed' David Hare

WAKING LIONS
AYELET GUNDAR-GOSHEN

'A literary thriller that is used as a vehicle to explore big
moral issues. I loved everything about it' *Daily Mail*

FOR A LITTLE WHILE
RICK BASS

'Bass is, hands down, a master of the short form, creating in a few pages
a natural world of mythic proportions' *New York Times Book Review*